# BIRDS OF
# SOUTHWESTERN BRITISH COLUMBIA

# BIRDS OF SOUTHWESTERN BRITISH COLUMBIA

Richard Cannings
Tom Aversa
Hal Opperman

Heritage House
VANCOUVER • VICTORIA • CALGARY

*For Jamie Smith (R.J.C.)*
*For Frances and Salvatore (T.A.)*
*For Luke and Isabelle (H.O.)*

Heritage House Publishing Company Ltd.
#108 – 17665 66A Avenue
Surrey, BC  V3S 2A7
www.heritagehouse.ca

**Library and Archives Canada Cataloguing in Publication**
Cannings, Richard J. (Richard James)
    Birds of southwestern British Columbia / Richard Cannings, Tom Aversa and Hal Opperman.

Includes index.
    ISBN 1-894384-96-2

    1. Birds—British Columbia—Lower Mainland—Identification. 2. Birds—British Columbia—Pacific Coast—Identification. 3. Birds—British Columbia—Vancouver Island—Identification.
I. Aversa, Tom, 1957–   II. Opperman, Hal N., 1938–   III. Title.
QL685.5.B7C38 2005        598'.09711'3          C2005-904619-8

Edited by Hal Opperman.
Book design by Gina Calle, CrespoCompany.com.
Cover design by Frances Hunter.
Front-cover photo of Pileated Woodpecker by Gloria Hopkins.
Back-cover photo of Varied Thrush by Ralph Hocken.
Printed in Hong Kong.

# Acknowledgements

Creating a bird identification guide is a significant undertaking and would not be possible without the contribution of many local birders. Dave Fraser, Hue MacKenzie, Wayne Weber, and Bruce Whittington generously shared their expertise with us on birds and birdwatching in the southwestern British Columbia region.

Thanks to Bob Morse and the R. W. Morse Company for providing a prototype for the book and collaborating with Heritage House on this project. Thanks also to Gina Calle of Crespo Company for her creative design elements, and to Bruce Whittington for his well-written foreword.

We owe a great debt to the many photographers who have provided photographs for this book, consistently meeting the challenge of capturing a bird's key field marks in photographs of high technical and artistic merit. Their names are listed on pages 402–404. In particular, Ralph Hocken, Laure Wilson Neish, Michael Shepard, Brian Small, and Hank Tseng spent many hours searching for just the right images for us. Special thanks to Gloria Hopkins for permission to use her photo of a Pileated Woodpecker on the front cover and Ralph Hocken for permission to use the Varied Thrush on the back cover.

A number of contributors who aided in the

publication of two related books, *Birds of the Puget Sound Region* and *Birds of the Willamette Valley Region*, are not listed here but again are recognized, since their contributions have been integral to *Birds of Southwestern British Columbia*.

Finally, thanks to Shawn Morse for the map of the southwestern British Columbia region, and to Eric Kraig for his bird drawings.

The success of this guide is the success of all those who have contributed to it. Their participation is sincerely appreciated.

# Contents

# Southwestern British Columbia

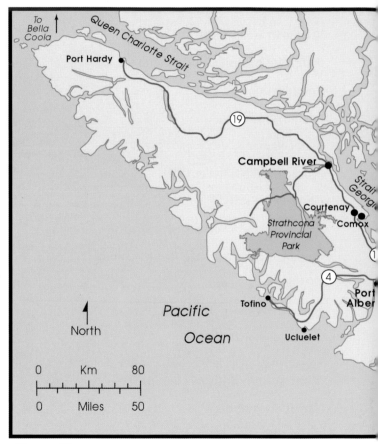

**Shawn Morse**

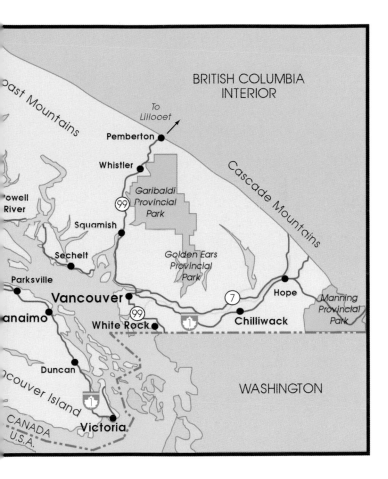

BRITISH COLUMBIA
INTERIOR

Coast Mountains

To
Lillooet

Pemberton

Whistler

Cascade Mountains

Powell
River

Garibaldi
Provincial
Park

(99)

Squamish

Sechelt

Golden Ears
Provincial
Park

Parksville

Vancouver

Hope

Manning
Provincial
Park

Nanaimo

(99)

White Rock

(7)

Chilliwack

Duncan

WASHINGTON

Vancouver Island

CANADA
U.S.A.

Victoria

# Common Local Birds

Here are some of the most common birds in southwestern British Columbia. For more information about each bird, go to its Species Account.

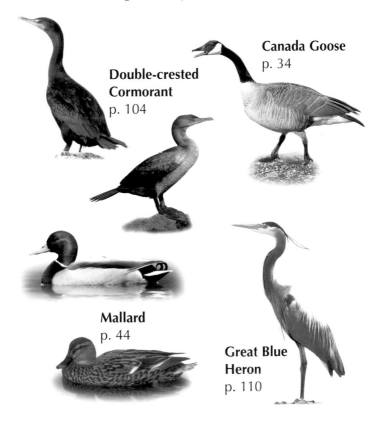

**Canada Goose**
p. 34

**Double-crested Cormorant**
p. 104

**Mallard**
p. 44

**Great Blue Heron**
p. 110

**Red-tailed Hawk**
p. 124

**Rock Pigeon**
p. 204

**Northwestern Crow**
p. 268

**Glaucous-winged Gull**
p. 190

**Rufous Hummingbird**
p. 232

**Northern Flicker**
p. 242

**Steller's Jay**
p. 266

**Barn Swallow**
p. 284

**Violet-green Swallow**
p. 278

**Downy Woodpecker**
p. 238

**Chestnut-backed Chickadee** p. 288

**Black-capped Chickadee** p. 286

**Red-breasted Nuthatch** p. 292

**Bushtit** p. 290

**Bewick's Wren** p. 296

**American Robin** p. 314

**European Starling**
p. 318

**Dark-eyed Junco**
p. 358

**House Finch**
p. 374

**Spotted Towhee**
p. 342

**Song Sparrow**
p. 350

xv

**Red-winged Blackbird**
p. 362

**Pine Siskin**
p. 378

**American Goldfinch**
p. 380

**House Sparrow**
p. 384

# Foreword

Over the years, I have accumulated dozens of bird books from many parts of the world, detailing the plumages of thousands of species of birds. There is one book, though, that I have used far more than any of the others. It is a sorry sight, its cloth-bound corners frayed and bent, and its spine replaced with a hurried application of duct tape. The book is my old "Peterson": Roger Tory Peterson's *Field Guide to Western Birds*. I mention it not because it is the best bird book in the world, but because it is the book that first introduced me to the magic of the birds in my backyard. In those days, there were few choices for a person just starting to learn about birds, and although the guides by Peterson and others were well done, more than a few novice birders shied away from the small illustrations and field-guide format.

For many people, the introduction to birding comes with the birds visiting their gardens or feeders, or those they see on their daily walks along the varied shores of southwestern British Columbia. These birds are common, for the most part, but to awakening eyes they are new and beautiful and fascinating to watch. More and more people every year become interested in birds and soon take the next step—learning to identify the ones they see.

This step usually involves purchasing a bird book. But which one? In my time as a bookseller specializing in natural history, I have seen thousands of books, an array bewildering enough to deter the most curious mind. Many field guides are now so comprehensive or advanced that they intimidate novice birders. "Beginner" books satisfy the need for a short time, but even casual birders outgrow these guides quickly. There has long been a need for a guide that provides good identification information on the birds most likely to be seen by birders in southwestern British Columbia.

*Birds of Southwestern British Columbia* fills the gap well. The photographs are excellent and illustrate the birds in the plumages most likely to be seen in the region, and it covers more than 200 species. It is a book that beginners as well as birders new to the region will find easy to use and will return to often.

Some guides organize birds in groups by colour or habitat. This system breaks down when birders expand their libraries to include other guides, which are often laid out according to a generally accepted scientific order. *Birds of Southwestern British Columbia* is laid out in the same way as most of the more advanced guides, so birders who choose to expand their horizons in future will find an easy transition to other guides.

The authors bring the wealth of their collective experience to this book, and the result is a guide that combines the best in identification tools with unparalleled regional knowledge.

I regard this book with a combination of wistfulness and envy. It reminds me of the thrill I felt when I identified my first Spotted Towhee in the backyard. I wish this book had been on the kitchen table to help with the identification. For those of you who have a world of birds yet to explore, there is a lifetime of opportunities ahead of you, and this book will make your discoveries much more rewarding.

*Bruce Whittington*
*Naturalist, veteran birder, and author of* Seasons With Birds

# Introduction

Birdwatching, or birding, has become one of Canada's most popular outdoor activities. It is estimated that one-fifth of all North Americans—50 million people—either watch or feed birds. Birding can be great family entertainment. It is easy to get started, inexpensive, healthy, and allows us to understand and appreciate the natural world. *Birds of Southwestern British Columbia* is for beginning birdwatchers who wish to identify the regularly occurring birds of the region. This guide will also appeal to experienced birders who wish to learn more about the behaviour, habitats, and seasonal occurrence of our local birds.

Given the popularity of birdwatching and the region's beauty, it is little wonder that the people of southwestern British Columbia enjoy seeing and studying the rich variety of our local birdlife. Over 200 species of birds are permanent residents or regular annual visitors. These are the birds featured in this guide. Those that can readily be found in the lowlands receive full Species Accounts. An additional 12 species likely to be encountered at higher elevations of the Cascade and Coast mountains are illustrated and briefly discussed in a special section on Mountain Specialties, while 12 more species that can be seen on boat trips off the west coast of Vancouver Island are included in a special section on Offshore Specialties.

## GEOGRAPHICAL COVERAGE

*Birds of Southwestern British Columbia* covers the south coast of the province and adjoining waters, including Vancouver Island, the Lower Mainland, Juan de Fuca,

Georgia, and Queen Charlotte straits, the central coast north to Bella Coola, and the Cascade and Coast mountains east to Manning Park and Whistler. The term "region," as used in the guide, refers to this entire geographical area, as depicted on the map on pages viii–ix.

## CONSERVATION

Increased development of the region's urban and rural communities has led to changes in habitat and habitat loss, impacting our local bird populations. Pollution of the Strait of Georgia waters by farms, pulp mills, sewage, marinas, garbage dumps, and storm runoff has had a direct effect on the region's water birds. Some populations have seen declines of up to 80 percent over the last 20 years. Deforestation has also taken its toll, as has urban and suburban sprawl. A diverse and thriving birdlife is an excellent indicator of a healthy environment. Those who enjoy birds should do all they can to protect birds and their habitats. We urge you to join one of the many conservation organizations such as local naturalists clubs (http://www.naturalists.bc.ca/), the Wild Bird Trust of British Columbia (http://www.wildbirdtrust.org), The Nature Trust of British Columbia (http://www.naturetrust.bc.ca/), The Land Conservancy (http://www.conservancy.bc.ca/), the Georgia Strait Alliance (http://www.georgiastrait.org), or the British Columbia Waterfowl Society (http://www.reifelbird sanctuary.com/bcws2.html), that strive to address and improve environmental conditions.

# Identifying Birds

It can be confusing when you first start trying to identify birds. First, look at the general shape, size, and colour of the bird. Check the Common Local Birds (pages xi–xvi) and see if it is there. If not, scan through the Species Account pages. Read the description—especially the **boldfaced** text—to see how it matches your bird. Compare range, similar species, and habitat. Keep comparing until you have a match.

The different colours of a bird's feathering ("plumage") and bare parts (bill, legs, feet) provide one of the best ways to identify a bird. Most of the plumages and colour patterns for each bird species are unique. However, plumages may vary within the same species between the sexes, between adults and younger birds, and by season.

In some species the male and the female have distinctly different plumages. Good examples are Mallard, House Finch, Red-winged Blackbird, and Rufous Hummingbird. Usually the males have more brilliant colours, as in these examples, while the females have muted colours. Other species such as Rock Pigeon, Steller's Jay, Northwestern Crow, and Song Sparrow show no plumage differences between the sexes.

Most birds seen in southwestern British Columbia in spring and summer display what is known as their summer or "breeding" plumage. Birds seen here in winter are usually in their "non-breeding" or winter plumage. Typically, but not always, the breeding plumage is more colourful or highly patterned and the non-breeding plumage is more muted.

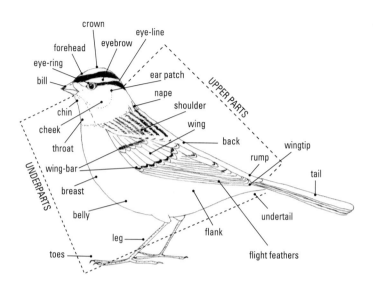

crown

eye-line

forehead eyebrow

eye-ring

bill ear patch

nape UPPER PARTS

chin shoulder

cheek wing

throat back

wingtip

wing-bar rump

UNDERPARTS tail

breast

belly undertail

leg flank

toes flight feathers

---

**Parts of a Bird.** It is helpful to know the names of the different parts of a bird. These sketches of a White-crowned Sparrow and an in-flight Mallard show the terms used to describe bird anatomy in this guide.

---

Moulting is the process of replacing worn feathers with new, fresh feathers. Most local birds replace some or all of their feathers in a moult in summer or early fall when they change into their non-breeding plumage. Most birds moult again in late winter or spring as they change into their breeding plumage. These moults occur over a period of several weeks or months.

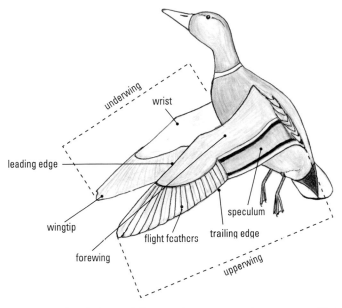

underwing

wrist

leading edge

wingtip

forewing

flight feathers

speculum

trailing edge

upperwing

Some birds have different plumages as they mature. This is particularly true for gulls, which take up to four years and several plumage stages to gain their adult plumage.

The term "juvenal plumage" refers to the plumage of a newborn bird after it loses its initial downy feathers. Some species hold this plumage for only a few weeks after fledging while others may hold it into winter. "First-year plumage" refers to the plumage held during the first 12 months of a bird's life. "Immature" refers to all plumages before the bird gains its adult plumage.

Colours and patterning may vary considerably among

birds of the same species and plumage stage, especially when they belong to different geographical populations. For instance, the Fox Sparrows that nest high in the Cascade and Coast mountains differ markedly in appearance from the ones that breed on the outer coast and winter throughout the lowlands of the region. Differences can be great even within the same local population. The majority of Red-tailed Hawks in southwestern British Columbia have light breasts and underwings, yet a certain percentage of birds have dark brown underparts and dark underwings with lighter-coloured flight feathers. Such consistently different types are called "colour morphs" (or just morphs).

In this book the birds are presented in family groupings, as shown in the Quick Guide to Local Birds on page 27. Learning the characteristics of the different bird families will make bird identification both easier and quicker. Birds in the same family look similar and often behave in a similar manner. Hummingbirds, for example, are all small, with long, thin bills, have fast wingbeats, and can hover. Once you see a bird with these characteristics, you are well on your way to identifying it as a hummingbird.

Don't expect every bird you see to look exactly like the photographs in this guide. Birds, like people, are individuals. To appreciate how variable birds of the same species can be, study the ones that come regularly to your backyard feeder. Male House Finches, for example, can show a wide range of coloration from rich, deep red to golden yellow. You may find that, with practice, you can learn to recognize individual birds by the subtle differences in their markings.

# Binoculars

Binoculars are a great help in getting good views of birds. Binoculars come in many sizes. Each is labelled with two numbers, e.g., 7 x 35, 8 x 40, 10 x 50. The first number is the magnification. You may think that the larger the magnification, the better the binocular. However, as magnification increases, clarity may diminish as well as field of view (the width of the area you can see at a given distance). Another trade-off is that the higher-powered binoculars are usually heavier, hence harder to hold steady or carry for extended periods of time.

The second number is the diameter of the big lens (objective) in millimetres. The larger the diameter, the greater the light-gathering capability of the binocular and the more colours and details you can see, especially in poor light conditions.

Many discount stores offer binoculars in the $75 to $150 price range, which may be suitable for beginning birders. Higher-quality binoculars are available at nature stores or camera shops and can cost from $250 to $2,000.

The best way to select a binocular is to go to a store that has a good selection and try out several. If you wear glasses, fold, screw, or snap down the eyecups to get your pupil closer to the lens so you get a larger image. Look at a sign at the other end of the store and see which binocular provides the sharpest image. There should be no distortion in either shape or colour. Which one feels more comfortable in the hand? Is it easy to change focus?

Can you focus on close objects (within three to four metres)? Which is the most durable and has the largest field of view?

Out in the field, examine what other birders are using and ask for the opportunity to look through their binoculars. Selecting a binocular is a personal thing—what is comfortable for you may not be for another birder. So, choose one that has sufficient magnification (7 or 8 power), a wide objective lens (40 millimetres or more), an acceptable field of view (100 metres or more at 1,000 metres), is easy to use, and fits your budget. A good rule of thumb is to buy the best binocular you can afford.

Also, make sure you get a wide binocular strap (at least 2.5 centimetres). It will help prevent a sore neck by the end of the day. Even better are some of the harnesses that transfer binocular weight to the shoulders rather than the neck. Binoculars also come with dust covers for each of the four lenses. Better-quality binoculars are waterproof, but in southwestern British Columbia it is nonetheless a good idea to make or purchase a removable rain guard to cover the small eyepieces so you do not have to wipe them dry all the time.

Finally, take time to pre-focus your binocular before using it. Do this by adjusting the central focus knob and the eyepiece focus until the image appears sharp through both lenses.

# Attracting Birds to Your Yard

Most people get involved in birdwatching by observing the birds that appear in their yards. Perhaps the easiest way to see birds is to put up feeders and watch for birds to appear. When they are perched and eating, birds tend to stay long enough for you to study the field marks at close range and identify the bird.

Although just hanging out a birdseed feeder will attract some birds, a complete backyard bird program has three important requirements: **food**, **water**, and **shelter**. By careful attention to all three of these elements you will not only increase the number and variety of birds that visit your yard, but you will also be contributing to their well-being. Many helpful books and brochures on bird feeding, nest boxes, and gardening for wildlife are available at nature stores and nurseries.

## FOOD

The food that birds eat comes mainly from natural sources. Native and ornamental shrubs, trees, and other plants provide fruits, seeds, flowers, and insects. You will attract more birds to your yard by selecting plants favourable to birds.

You may also provide seed, suet, and other products to entice birds to your yard. Many seeds are suitable for feeding birds although the best product for our region is black-oil sunflower seed, which has high fat content.

Many grocery and hardware stores sell a birdseed mix that contains some black-oil sunflower seed but often has a lot of millet (the small, round, tan-coloured seed) and filler grains. When you place this seed in a hanging feeder some of the birds will eat only the sunflower seed and will kick the filler and millet to the ground. In elevated feeders, it is much better to use only black-oil sunflower seed or a specialized mix of seed that is high in nutritional value.

Different birds have different feeding preferences. You may wish to try more than one of the following common feeder types, depending on the species of birds you wish to attract.

- **Fly-through and hopper feeders** are hung or mounted on a pole or deck, normally about 1.5–1.8 metres above the ground. Stocked with black-oil sunflower seed, they attract Steller's Jay, finches, Red-breasted Nuthatch, and chickadees.

- A **ground feeder or platform feeder** is placed near the ground or up to table height and filled with millet, corn, or a birdseed mix that has some black-oil sunflower seeds but is mostly millet. This feeder will attract doves, pigeons, ducks, sparrows, Dark-eyed Junco, Spotted Towhee, and Red-winged Blackbird. Buy a ground feeder with a bottom screen that allows the rain to drain through.

- Cylindrical **tube feeders** are either hung or mounted and can be filled with a nutritional mix of birdseed or just black-oil sunflower seed. They attract the smaller birds such as Red-breasted Nuthatch, Pine Siskin, chickadees, and finches.

- A specialized tube feeder to hold niger thistle seed is called a **thistle** or **finch feeder** and can attract numbers of finches like House Finch, Pine Siskin, and American Goldfinch.

- **Suet**, either acquired at a local meat market or purchased at the nature store in suet cakes, attracts woodpeckers, Red-breasted Nuthatch, chickadees, Bushtit, and a host of other birds seeking its high-energy fat.

- Red **hummingbird feeders** attract Rufous and Anna's Hummingbirds that breed in southwestern British Columbia. It is easy to make hummingbird nectar: mix one part sugar to four parts water, boil, let cool, and then fill your feeders. Do not add any artificial food colouring; the red of the feeder is sufficient to attract hummingbirds.

Experiment with your feeder locations and different birdseed to learn what works best in your yard. Feeders should be placed close to natural shelters such as bushes and trees so the birds can escape from predators. You can feed the birds all year long without worrying that your bird feeding will delay the birds' migration. They will leave when the time is right.

## WATER

Birds need water for bathing and drinking. You will find that you attract more birds if you offer a reliable source of clean water in your yard. Consider placing a concrete birdbath filled with two or three centimetres of water to meet their needs. Clean and refill it regularly. Be sure the bottom surface is rough so the birds can get a good footing. Place the birdbath near shrubs or trees where they can preen after bathing and escape from predators. Try adding a dripper to the birdbath. The sound of dripping water attracts birds.

## SHELTER AND NEST BOXES

Birds need cover so they can seek protection from bad weather and predators. Nearby bushes, shrubs, and trees will help meet their needs as will a loosely stacked brush pile. Neighbourhood cats can be a real problem, especially when they lurk beneath feeders and birdbaths. Careful placement or screening off of feeders and birdbaths, or placing chicken wire strategically in front of favourite cat-stalking areas, will help protect the birds.

Some of the birds featured in this guide are cavity-nesters and may be enticed to use a birdhouse that you can either build yourself or purchase at a nature store. It is important to realize that there is no such thing as a generic nest box. Different birds have different needs, and each nest box has to meet the demands of its occupant or it will not be used. The size of the opening and its height above the floor are critical, as is the height of the nest box above the ground. Some nest boxes also serve as wintering roosting boxes for the smaller birds. It may take a season or two to attract chickadees, nuthatches, or swallows to your nest boxes. Once they start nesting on your property, you will enjoy watching the behaviour of these nesting birds.

## HYGIENE

Feeders, the ground below the feeders, and birdbaths need to be cleaned on a regular basis to eliminate the possibility of the spread of avian diseases. Scrub the feeders and birdbaths with soap and water. Mix one part bleach to 10 parts hot water to sanitize them. Rinse them well then let them dry completely before refilling.

Be sure to inspect nest boxes each fall and give them a good cleaning, but use no insecticides. Discard used nesting materials. Repair any damage so the boxes are ready and waiting for their new occupants to arrive in spring.

# Observing Birds

Many birdwatchers are quite content just to watch the birds in their yards casually. Some, however, get more involved and begin to look for birds beyond their immediate neighbourhood. To get the most out of birding in the field, look, listen, and move slowly. Try to keep conversations to a minimum.

To help locate birds, watch for their movement and listen for their calls. Most often we see birds fly to a nearby branch or flit around in a tree. Their movement catches our attention. But an important part of birdwatching is listening and, many times, it is its song or call that draws us to the bird.

Bird songs are a good way to identify birds. Each bird species has a unique song, and, with practice, you can learn to differentiate the songs. You can purchase tapes or CDs that allow you to study bird vocalizations at your leisure. With experience, you will be able to identify birds simply by their songs and calls.

## WHEN TO GO BIRDING

Small birds tend to be most active when they are feeding early in the morning (as early as daybreak). Shorebirds tend be most active while they are feeding on incoming and outgoing tides; they often rest at high tides. Hawks become active in the morning after the rising temperature creates thermals that allow them to soar through the air. Most owls are nocturnal and are most active in the evening or just before dawn.

Southwestern British Columbia birds vary with the season. Some species stay in the region throughout the year while others arrive in the spring and leave in the fall. Other species migrate into the lowlands of our area from the north, the mountains, or the interior of the continent and spend the winter.

Spring is a great time of year. The flowers are blossoming, the trees are getting their buds, and the birds, in their bright breeding plumages, return from their wintering grounds. The males start singing and the local nesting birds seek mates, breed, and start to raise their families. Hummingbirds feed on flower nectar or at feeders. Wintering birds head north to their breeding grounds.

In summer, the local young birds hatch, and their parents are busy feeding them. As summer progresses, the young learn to fly and fend for themselves. By August, summer visitors are beginning to head south for their wintering grounds.

By late summer, most of the Arctic-breeding shorebirds have passed through on their way south. As fall changes to winter, flocks of waterfowl appear on our lakes and ponds. Dunlins arrive to winter on local mud flats. Our resident birds continue to use neighbourhood bird feeders, joined by winter visitors driven down to the lowlands by snowfall in the mountains.

## KEEPING RECORDS

Some people keep a checklist of all the birds that appear in their yard ("yard list") or of all the birds seen in their lifetime ("life list"). As lists grow, so does a sense of personal accomplishment. Along with the pleasure of finding new and different birds comes an incentive to learn more about them. Many dedicated birdwatchers keep a detailed journal of what they see, when and where, and the birds' behaviours. Careful record keeping by knowledgeable observers can contribute greatly to scientific understanding of birdlife.

A checklist of the local birds is provided on pages 405–411. Naturalist clubs, parks, and nature sanctuaries often produce checklists for local areas. Inquire about these at nature stores and visitor centres.

# Bird Habitats in Southwestern British Columbia

The place where a bird or other living creature is normally found is termed its "habitat." Birds are quite diverse in their habitat requirements. Brown Creepers are seldom seen over open salt water, or loons in trees. To a large extent, the secret to finding and identifying birds is knowing the habitats and developing an understanding of which birds are likely to be seen where. The more types of habitat you explore, the greater the variety of birds you will see.

Southwestern British Columbia has 12 major habitat categories:

## OFFSHORE MARINE WATERS

These waters are open-ocean areas off the west coast of Vancouver Island and the central coast. Albatrosses, shearwaters, fulmars, and storm-petrels forage here. Alcids such as Cassin's Auklet, Ancient Murrelet, Rhinoceros Auklet, and Tufted Puffin feed offshore as well, especially in the non-breeding seasons. California and Sabine's Gulls, Black-legged Kittiwake, Pomarine and Parasitic Jaegers, Arctic Tern, and Red and Red-necked Phalaropes all move through these offshore waters on their annual migrations.

## PROTECTED MARINE WATERS

This habitat includes all the salt water of the Strait of Georgia and adjoining inlets, bays, passages, and straits.

Protected marine waters are host to loons, grebes, cormorants, scaups, scoters, goldeneyes, gulls, terns, and alcids. Purple Martins nest locally in a few saltwater bays. There are many vantage points from which to scan saltwater habitats including Clover Point in Victoria, the Iona Island Jetty in Richmond, and the Stanley Park seawall in Vancouver.

## Rocky Shore

The rocky shore habitat includes cobbled beaches, breakwaters, and rocky outcroppings along the saltwater shoreline. Clover Point in Victoria, Lighthouse Park in West Vancouver, the Tsawwassen Ferry Terminal, and many other similar sites along the coast attract a selection of birds that prefer this habitat, including cormorants, Black Oystercatcher, turnstones, and Surfbird, while Harlequin Ducks tend to feed in the waters off these shores.

## Sandy Shore, Mud Flats, and Salt Marsh

The extensive mud flats and marshes of the Fraser Delta are among the most important areas for migrant and wintering water birds in Canada, hosting huge numbers of Snow Geese, American Wigeons, Northern Pintails, Western Sandpipers, Dunlins, and many other species. Eelgrass beds along the east coast of Vancouver Island are vital in spring for large numbers of migrating Brant. Estuaries throughout the region are home to wintering Trumpeter Swans and breeding Purple Martins.

## Fresh Water, Marsh, and Shore

Lakes and freshwater marshes are not common in southwestern British Columbia, but are disproportionately important for many birds. Some examples are Cheam Lake, Harrison Bay, Lost Lagoon, Elk Lake, and Somenos Lake. Great Blue Heron, Bald Eagle, Osprey, and Belted Kingfisher fish in these waters, and water birds such as grebes, geese, ducks, and coots may be found there. American Bittern, Green Heron, and Virginia Rail skulk in marsh vegetation. Cattails often support nesting Marsh Wrens and Red-winged Blackbirds. Swallows catch insects over the water, while songbirds such as Yellow Warbler frequent the trees and bushes along the water's edges, foraging for food.

## Wet Coniferous Forest

This habitat includes coniferous forests at low and middle elevations, dominated by Douglas-fir, western hemlock, and western redcedar. These woods are home to Band-tailed Pigeon, several owls, Hairy Woodpecker, Hammond's Flycatcher, Steller's Jay, Chestnut-backed Chickadee, Winter Wren, Golden-crowned Kinglet, Varied Thrush, Western Tanager, Yellow-rumped Warbler, and Pine Siskin. At higher elevations, forests of amabilis fir, mountain hemlock, and subalpine fir host Blue Grouse, Red-breasted Sapsucker, Gray Jay, Hermit Thrush, and Townsend's Warbler.

## Broadleaf Forest

This habitat includes stands of red alder, black cottonwood, bigleaf and vine maple, and arbutus.

Extensive broadleaf woodlands line the riparian zone along many creeks and larger streams throughout southwestern British Columbia, most notably in the Fraser Valley. Broadleaf trees often grow in mixed stands with conifers as well as in uniform stands after the logging of coniferous forests. The birds that prefer this habitat include Ruffed Grouse, Western Screech and Barred Owls, Downy Woodpecker, Western Wood-Pewee, Pacific-slope Flycatcher, Hutton's, Warbling, and Red-eyed Vireos, Black-capped Chickadee, and Black-throated Gray and Wilson's Warblers.

## GARRY-OAK SAVANNAS

This small, threatened habitat occurs in the Gulf Islands and the coastal lowlands of southeastern Vancouver Island—some of the driest parts of the region. It is characterized by native grasslands and scattered stands of Garry oak. Birds to be found in such places include California Quail, Common Nighthawk, House Wren, Chipping Sparrow, and (formerly) Western Bluebird and Western Meadowlark.

## SUBALPINE PARKLAND AND ALPINE MEADOWS

This high-elevation, open habitat of the Cascades, Coast, and Vancouver Island mountains consists of meadows with alpine wildflowers and scattered stands of trees. Look here for White-tailed Ptarmigan, Horned Lark, Mountain Bluebird, American Pipit, and Gray-crowned Rosy-Finch. Strathcona, Manning, and Garibaldi provincial parks offer good access to this habitat, as do Mount Arrowsmith and the Whistler-Blackcomb ski area.

## SHRUBBY THICKETS

Shrubby thickets exist in clearings and around the edges of coniferous and broadleaf woods, transportation and power-line corridors, and overgrown fencerows. Willow Flycatcher, Bushtit, Bewick's Wren, Orange-crowned and MacGillivray's Warblers, Spotted Towhee, and sparrows live in this habitat.

## PARKS AND GARDENS

This urban and suburban habitat attracts many of the birds that come to our backyard bird feeders, including hummingbirds, woodpeckers, chickadees, Red-breasted Nuthatch, grosbeaks, Purple and House Finches, and American Goldfinch. This habitat also hosts Rock Pigeon, Northwestern Crow, American Robin, European Starling, and House Sparrow.

## FARMLAND AND PASTURES

The open pastures and agricultural fields of the lowlands host Northern Harrier, Ring-necked Pheasant, Mourning Dove, Short-eared Owl, and many wintering geese, swans, ducks, hawks, eagles, falcons, gulls, starlings, and blackbirds. Prime examples of farmlands are found throughout the lower Fraser Valley, the Fraser Delta, and the Martindale Flats in Saanich.

# Birding in Southwestern British Columbia

One of the best ways to see new birds is to join the local naturalist club on a field trip. Participants often visit new areas, learn how to identify new birds, and meet people who share a common interest.

After studying the birds in your yard, visit local parks and greenbelts. A selection of top birding locations in southwestern British Columbia is listed below. For maps and directions to these and other fine regional birding sites, consult the birdfinding guides and other resources listed on pages 24–26.

**Greater Vancouver**   Stanley Park, Jericho Beach, Lighthouse Park, Cypress Provincial Park, Iona Island, Roberts Bank, Boundary Bay, Blackie Spit, Campbell Valley Park, Minnekhada Park, Pitt River marshes

**Fraser Valley**   Harrison Bay, Cheam Lake, Chilliwack River

**Squamish-Whistler**  Squamish River estuary, Brackendale (for Bald Eagles in midwinter), Whistler-Blackcomb (alpine species), Garibaldi Provincial Park

**Sunshine Coast**  Mission Point/Davis Bay, Roberts Creek estuary, Sechelt Marsh, Sargeant Bay Park, Smugglers Cove Park, Tetrahedron Park

**Greater Victoria**   Clover Point, Island View Beach, Martindale Flats, Esquimalt Lagoon, Witty's Lagoon, East Sooke Park (fall raptor migration)

**Duncan**   Cowichan Bay, Quamichan Lake, Somenos Lake/Flats, Duncan Sewage Lagoons

**Nanaimo-Parksville-Qualicum**   Nanaimo River estuary, Buttertubs Marsh, Piper's Lagoon, Nanoose Bay, Rathtrevor Park, Mount Arrowsmith

**Comox Valley**   Baynes Sound, Courtenay River estuary, Mansfield Road Slough, Mount Washington

**Campbell River**   Discovery Passage, Miracle Beach Park, Strathcona Park

**Northern Vancouver Island**   Salmon River estuary, Queen Charlotte Sound/Johnstone Strait

**West Coast Vancouver Island**   Grice Bay, La Perouse Bank (offshore species), J.V. Clyne Nature Sanctuary

# Helpful Resources

There are a number of ways to get additional information about birds and their habitats, bird identification, and good places to go birding. Some of the best information is available through books, birding organizations, websites, and local nature stores. Here are some of our favourites:

## REGIONAL PUBLICATIONS

Keith Taylor. 2000. *The Birder's Guide: Vancouver Island*, 5th ed. Vancouver: Steller Press.

Vancouver Natural History Society. 2001. *The Birder's Guide to Vancouver and the Lower Mainland*. Vancouver/Toronto/New York: Whitecap Books.

R. Wayne Campbell, Neil K. Dawe, Ian McTaggart-Cowan, John M. Cooper, Gary W. Kaiser, Michael C. E. McNall, G.E. John Smith, and Andrew C. Stewart. 1990–2001. *The Birds of British Columbia*. 4 vols. Victoria: Royal British Columbia Museum, and Vancouver/Toronto: University of British Columbia Press.

Richard and Sydney Cannings. 1996. *British Columbia: A Natural History*. Vancouver: Greystone Books.

Richard and Sydney Cannings. 2002. *The B.C. Roadside Naturalist*. Vancouver: Greystone Books.

## IDENTIFICATION GUIDES

David Allen Sibley. 2003. *The Sibley Field Guide to Birds of Western North America*. New York: Alfred A. Knopf.

*Field Guide to the Birds of North America*, 4th ed. 2002. Washington, D.C.: National Geographic Society.

Kenn Kaufman. 2000. *Birds of North America*. New York: Houghton Mifflin.

Roger Tory Peterson. 1990. *A Field Guide to Western Birds*, 3rd ed. Boston: Houghton Mifflin.

## OTHER REGIONAL BIRDING RESOURCES

There are 24 local naturalist clubs in southwestern British Columbia. They provide an excellent means to learn more about birds. Most clubs have a newsletter, meetings, and local field trips to search for birds. Some have websites with information of interest to birdwatchers. For details, visit the Federation of British Columbia Naturalists' website at http://www.naturalists.bc.ca/.

The Vancouver Natural History Society website has directions to over 30 birding sites in the Lower Mainland. Visit http://www.naturalhistory.bc.ca/vnhs/ and follow links to "Birding."

The British Columbia Field Ornithologists (BCFO)—

open to all persons interested in birds—offers field trips, a newsletter and journal, and an annual conference. Visit the BCFO website at http://www.bcfo.ca/ for information on membership and upcoming activities.

Kevin Slagboom's "Birding in British Columbia" website (http://www.birding.bc.ca/) offers a great deal of useful information on local birding as well as links to other sites.

Three e-mail lists on birds and birding in southwestern British Columbia are bcbirdingvanisland, bcvanbirds, and bcbirds. All can be joined on-line at http://groups.yahoo.com.

## NATURE STORES

There are a number of good nature stores in southwestern British Columbia. Their staffs are always eager to answer your bird and bird-feeding questions. The yellow pages of the telephone directory will locate the closest nature store.

# Quick Guide to Local Birds

This guide is organized by families so related species are shown together, with a few birds found primarily in the mountains or on offshore trips grouped at the end. The Species Account pages are colour-coded and thumb-indexed in the following manner:

WATERFOWL (Geese, Swans, Dabbling Ducks)

WATERFOWL (Diving Ducks)

UPLAND GAME BIRDS (Pheasant, Grouse, Quail)—LOONS—GREBES—CORMORANTS—WADING BIRDS (Bittern, Herons)

VULTURE—DIURNAL RAPTORS (Eagle, Hawks, Falcons)

RAIL AND COOT—SHOREBIRDS (Plovers, Oystercatcher, Sandpipers, Whimbrel, Turnstone, Dowitchers, Snipe, Phalarope)

JAEGER, GULLS, AND TERNS—ALCIDS (Murre, Guillemot, Murrelet, Auklet)

PIGEONS AND DOVE—OWLS—NIGHTHAWK—SWIFTS

HUMMINGBIRDS—KINGFISHER—WOODPECKERS—FLYCATCHERS (Wood-Pewee, Flycatchers)

SHRIKE—VIREOS—CORVIDS (Jay, Crow, Raven)—SWALLOWS (Martin, Swallows)

CHICKADEES—BUSHTIT—NUTHATCH—CREEPER—WRENS—DIPPER—KINGLETS—THRUSHES (Thrushes, Robin)

STARLING—PIPIT—WAXWING—WARBLERS—TANAGER

NATIVE SPARROWS (Towhee, Sparrows, Junco)—BLACK-HEADED GROSBEAK

BLACKBIRDS (Blackbirds, Meadowlark, Cowbird, Oriole)—FINCHES (Finches, Crossbill, Siskin, Evening Grosbeak)—HOUSE SPARROW

MOUNTAIN SPECIALTIES

OFFSHORE SPECIALTIES

# Species Accounts

The following pages present accounts and photographs of the most familiar bird species of southwestern British Columbia. Information on each species is presented in a standardized format: see the sample page (opposite) for an explanation. Species are grouped by families, colour-coded and thumb-indexed. A dozen species commonest in the mountains are presented separately at the end (pages 386–393) as are another 12 found mostly in offshore waters west of Vancouver Island (pages 394–401). The Quick Guide on page 27 of the book will help you locate the birds.

The following terms are used to describe the relative abundance of each species and the likelihood of finding it in a particular season. These definitions were developed by the American Birding Association.

- **Common:** Found in moderate to large numbers, and easily found in appropriate habitat at the right time of year.
- **Fairly Common:** Found in small to moderate numbers, and usually easy to find in appropriate habitat at the right time of year.
- **Uncommon:** Found in small numbers, and usually—but not always—found with some effort in appropriate habitat at the right time of year.
- **Rare:** Occurs annually in very small numbers. Not to be expected on any given day, but may be found with extended effort over the course of the appropriate season(s).

Birds shown in the photographs in the Species Accounts are adults unless the captions indicate otherwise.

## NAME OF THE SPECIES
### *Its scientific (Latin) name*

**Description:** Length (and wingspan for larger species), followed by a description that includes differences in plumages between sexes and ages. Key field marks—unique markings visible in the field that help distinguish one species from another—are shown in **boldfaced** type.

**Similar Species:** Identifies similar-appearing species and describes how to tell them apart.

**Seasonal Abundance:** Identifies the times of year that the species is here and its relative abundance (see facing page for definitions of abundance terms). Also describes its overall range.

**Where to Find:** Explains generally where this bird may be found in southwestern British Columbia; may also suggest some of the better locations to search for it.

**Habitat:** Describes the habitat(s) in which this bird is normally found in southwestern British Columbia.

**Diet and Behaviour:** Identifies the prime sources of food and highlights behaviours characteristic of this species.

**Voice:** Describes the main song and calls of the species.

**Did you know?** Provides interesting facts about this species.

**Date and Location Seen:** A place for you to record the date and location of your first sighting of this species.

**Description:** 71 cm, wingspan 137 cm. White goose with **black wingtips**, pinkish legs, **pink bill with blackish "grinning patch."** Dark variant called Blue Goose (rare in region) grey with white head, neck. JUVENILE: Dusky upperparts, greyish legs.

**Similar Species:** Swans larger without black wingtips. Ross's Goose (not shown; rare in region) smaller with stubby bill.

**Seasonal Abundance:** Common but local winter resident on Lower Mainland, rare elsewhere in region; arrives late September, departs by early May. Breeds on Arctic tundra from northeastern Russia east to Greenland, winters to northern Mexico. Almost all birds wintering in region come from Wrangel Island, Siberia.

**Where to Find:** Local wintering grounds mostly limited to Fraser Delta; Reifel Bird Sanctuary best spot for viewing, but also seen at Iona Island, west dykes of Lulu Island. Migrants rare elsewhere in lowland fields.

**Habitat:** Estuaries, shortgrass or agricultural fields.

**Diet and Behaviour:** Forages mostly on land but also in shallow water, almost entirely on plant materials including grasses, shoots, waste grain. Highly gregarious. Noisy, single-species flocks number in tens of thousands, appear blizzard-like when flushed by marauding eagle

**Voice:** Highly vocal. Raucous, high-pitched, honking yelps.

**Did you know?** Snow Geese are often called "wavies" due to the undulating, irregular waves they form in flight.

**Date and Location Seen:** _____

Grey-bellied form

**Description:** 61 cm, wingspan 107 cm. Stocky, short-necked, **small-billed** goose, mostly blackish with black bill, legs; white rump, undertail; barred whitish flanks; **white neck-ring**. JUVENILE: Lacks neck-ring in fall.

**Similar Species:** Cackling Goose, Canada Goose (both page 35) with white chin patch; most races larger, with longer bill.

**Seasonal Abundance:** Common but very local winter resident in region; arrives November, departs by May. Numbers swelled by spring migrants, February–April. Breeds on high-latitude tundra in North America, Eurasia; winters mostly to temperate zone.

**Where to Find:** Inland marine waters, rarely seen away from salt water. Good locations include Tsawwassen ferry jetty, Boundary Bay Regional Park, Englishman River estuary at Parksville.

**Habitat:** Coastline, including bays, estuaries—often with gravel bottom.

**Diet and Behaviour:** Forages by grazing on tidal flats, wading, upending in water. Diet almost exclusively leafy marine vegetation such as eelgrass. Highly gregarious. Rarely flocks with other species although may use same habitats. Flies low over ocean in ragged lines.

**Voice:** Quietly murmured, nasal *rrok rrok.*

**Did you know?** Four recognized forms of this widely distributed goose may someday be considered separate species. Typical west-coast birds have dark bellies. West Atlantic birds are whiter below with a partial neck ring. A few birds seen in British Columbia have grey bellies; this population winters near Bellingham, Washington.

**Date and Location Seen:** _____

Canada Goose

Cackling Goose (right)

**Description:** Variable. Smallest Cackling 56 cm, wingspan 109 cm; largest Canada 109 cm, wingspan 152 cm. Both mostly greyish-brown with black legs, bill, tail; white rump, undertail; **black head, neck with white chin patch**.

**Similar Species:** Brant (page 33) lacks white chin patch. Greater White-fronted Goose (not shown; uncommon in region) has yellow legs, lacks chin patch.

**Seasonal Abundance:** CACKLING: Uncommon migrant, winter resident in region. CANADA: Common migrant, resident in region. Migratory races of both arrive by October, depart by May. Range throughout North America south to northern Mexico (Cackling mostly in West).

**Where to Find:** Throughout lowlands; less common to moderate elevations. Cackling usually with Canada flocks.

**Habitat:** Ponds, lakes, marshes, grassy fields, estuaries, rivers.

**Diet and Behaviour:** Forage mostly on land but also in water, primarily for plant materials. Canada did not formerly breed in region, but introduced populations have become habituated to humans, now thrive year round in urban, rural areas.

**Voice:** Honk; smaller races of Cackling higher-pitched yelping.

**Did you know?** Three races of Cackling Goose and four of Canada Goose occur in southwestern British Columbia. Small, dark, short-necked races of Cackling are easily distinguished from large, light-breasted races of Canada, but intermediate races can be difficult to separate.

**Date and Location Seen:** _____

Trumpeter Swan

Mute Swan

Tundra Swan

**Description:** 152 cm / 132 cm, wingspan 203 cm / 168 cm. Huge, white, **long-necked** waterfowl with black bill as adults, juvenile bill pinkish. TRUMPETER: Larger; long **black bill extends to eye in broad triangle**; juvenile retains grey plumage throughout spring. TUNDRA: Smaller; **bill tapers to thin horizontal line at eye**; usually patch of yellow skin below eye; **juvenile white by spring**.

**Similar Species:** Snow Goose (page 31) smaller, has black wingtips. Introduced **Mute Swan** (see inset; small breeding population on southern Vancouver Island) has **orange bill with black knob at base**.

**Seasonal Abundance:** TRUMPETER common, TUNDRA uncommon winter residents in region (early November–March). TRUMPETER: Breeds south-central Alaska, other scattered locations in western North America. TUNDRA: Breeds on high tundra in Eurasia, North America, winters to temperate zone.

**Where to Find:** Coastal lowlands, farm fields of eastern Vancouver Island, Fraser Valley. Ten percent of world population of Trumpeter winters in Comox Valley.

**Habitat:** Ponds, estuaries, riverine marshes, agricultural fields.

**Diet and Behaviour:** Forage on plant materials on land or in water, often in flocks including both species.

**Voice:** TRUMPETER: Lower-pitched, like trumpet. TUNDRA: Gooselike barking *klow wow*.

**Did you know?** The Trumpeter Swan, close to extinction a century ago, is rapidly recovering.

**Date and Location Seen:** _____

Male

Female

# WOOD DUCK
*Aix sponsa*

**Description:** 43 cm, wingspan 76 cm. Unique, short-necked duck with long, broad tail, **swept-back crest**, white belly, dark blue speculum bordered at rear by white. MALE: Spectacularly **multicoloured**. Green head; white partial neck collar, face pattern; scarlet eye-ring, bill base. Dull in summer, retaining head pattern, red bill. FEMALE: Brownish with broad **teardrop-shaped eye-ring**.

**Similar Species:** Mandarin Duck (not shown; introduced from Asia, rare in region). Male gaudy with white face, orange "side-whiskers"; females closely similar but Mandarin with lighter head, upperparts; eye-ring smaller.

**Seasonal Abundance:** Fairly common summer resident in region; uncommon, local in winter (beginning October); migrants return March. Ranges across southern Canada, U.S.; winters to Mexico, Caribbean.

**Where to Find:** Low to moderate elevations; especially common central Fraser Valley; also Stanley Park, Duncan area.

**Habitat:** Wooded swamps, ponds; shady, slow rivers; rarely open lakes.

**Diet and Behaviour:** Forages mostly in water, seldom upending. Diet mainly seeds; takes more insects in summer. Nests in cavities; often seen on tree branches. Disperses late summer–fall, may gather in small groups outside nesting season.

**Voice:** Male gives thin, high whistles, female penetrating *ooo eeek* when flushed or alarmed.

**Did you know?** Threatened with extinction a century ago by overhunting, Wood Ducks have recovered, aided in part by placement of thousands of nest boxes.

**Date and Location Seen:** _____

Male

Female

**Description:** 48 cm, wingspan 84 cm. Medium-sized, rather plain dabbling duck with **white belly**, steep forehead, yellow feet, **white patch in speculum**. MALE: Mostly plain, variegated grey with back plumes, puffy head shape, dark bill, **black rump, undertail**; dull as female in summer. FEMALE: Mottled brown with yellowish-orange on sides of bill.

**Similar Species:** Female Mallard (page 45) longer, more bulky, lacks white speculum.

**Seasonal Abundance:** Common year-round resident in region. Ranges across North America, Eurasia in middle latitudes, winters to subtropics.

**Where to Find:** Throughout lowlands, especially on Fraser Delta.

**Habitat:** Ponds, lakes, marshes, estuaries. Prefers fresh water.

**Diet and Behaviour:** Forages primarily for plant material, dabbling at surface, upending, or occasionally grazing on land. Sociable, often flocking with other dabblers. Pair formation begins by fall.

**Voice:** Male with unique, low-pitched *reb reb* call, also squeaky whistle. Female gives nasal quack.

**Did you know?** In British Columbia, Gadwalls formerly bred only east of the Coast Range; small numbers began breeding on the Fraser Delta in 1966. Gadwalls now are locally common there and increasing on southern Vancouver Island.

**Date and Location Seen:** _____

Eurasian Wigeon
Male

American Wigeon
Male

American Wigeon
Female

**Description:** 48 cm, wingspan 81 cm. Short-necked dabbling ducks with **bluish-grey bill**, relatively long tail, **white forewing patch**. EURASIAN: **Grey sides**, white flanks, black undertail, **reddish head, yellowish forehead**. AMERICAN: Similar with **brownish sides, grey head, white forehead, green behind eye**. Females, summer males duller.

**Similar Species:** Gadwall (page 41) has white in speculum, not forewing; female has yellow on bill.

**Seasonal Abundance:** EURASIAN: Uncommon winter resident in region, in flocks of Americans (arrives later). Ranges across Eurasia, winters to tropics; some stray to North America. AMERICAN: Common winter resident in region, arrives late August, departs by May; very rare breeder. Breeds across North America, winters to Central America.

**Where to Find:** Widespread in lowlands; especially abundant Boundary Bay, Fraser Delta. Most large American Wigeon flocks hold one or more Eurasians.

**Habitat:** Ponds, marshes, bays, shortgrass fields, park lawns.

**Diet and Behaviour:** Eat mostly plant material. Graze more than other ducks. Forage in water by skimming surface, rarely upending; also steal plants from American Coots, diving ducks. Form large, tight flocks, especially on land.

**Voice:** Distinctive *wee whe whir* whistled by male; female with growling quack.

**Did you know?** Wigeons are called Baldpates by hunters.

**Date and Location Seen:** _____

Male

Female

**Description:** 56 cm, wingspan 89 cm. Large, **heavy-bodied** dabbling duck with orange legs, **blue speculum** bordered front, rear with white. MALE: **Iridescent green head**, greyish sides with darker back, chestnut breast, white neck-ring, yellow bill; in summer dull as female but retains greenish-yellow bill. FEMALE: Mottled brown with blotchy yellowish-orange bill.

**Similar Species:** In female-type plumage, told from other dabbling ducks by larger size, blue speculum.

**Seasonal Abundance:** Common resident in region; numbers augmented in winter with migrants from north. Ranges around northern hemisphere from Subarctic to subtropics.

**Where to Find:** Widespread in region, less common in mountains.

**Habitat:** Any fresh- or saltwater body, also farm fields, city parks.

**Diet and Behaviour:** Forages in water—upending, skimming near surface, even diving (rarely), mostly for plant but also for animal material. Grazes on land for waste grain, grass, insects. In parks becomes habituated to humans, takes handouts. Strong flyer. Gregarious, often flocking with other ducks. Pair formation, courtship begin in fall, nesting by late March.

**Voice:** Female makes familiar quacking. Male offers single whistles while courting, grating calls in aggression.

**Did you know?** Mallards are the origin of every variety of domestic duck except the Muscovy. Many strange-looking ducks in city parks are escaped farmyard Mallards.

**Date and Location Seen:** _____

**Blue-winged Teal Male**

**Blue-winged Teal Female**

**Cinnamon Teal Male**

**Description:** 38 cm, wingspan 58 cm. Small dabblers with **long, dark bill**, green speculum, **powder-blue forewing patch visible in flight**. BLUE-WINGED: Male brown with white flank patch, head grey with **bold white crescent behind bill**; dull as female summer–fall. Female mottled brown with diffuse pale facial area behind bill. CINNAMON: Male **chestnut-red** with red eye; dull as female summer–fall. Female mottled brown with plain face. Nearly impossible to distinguish juvenile Blue-winged from Cinnamon Teal, but latter averages longer bill, plainer face.

**Similar Species:** Green-winged Teal (page 53) smaller, shorter-billed, lacks blue forewing patch.

**Seasonal Abundance:** BLUE-WINGED: Uncommon breeder in region; much more common as late-May migrant. Ranges Alaska, Labrador south to Texas, winters south to Brazil. CINNAMON: Fairly common breeder, present in region from April through September; very rare in winter. Breeds western North America, winters south to Patagonia.

**Where to Find:** Mostly lowlands; sewage ponds particularly favoured.

**Habitat:** Prefer fresh water in open areas: ponds, marshes, flooded fields.

**Diet and Behaviour:** Both forage for plant, animal matter in shallows, rarely upending. Blue-winged eats more insects. Fast, agile fliers, frequently found in small groups of mixed species of teals.

**Voice:** Females quack; males chatter, whistle.

**Did you know?** Closely related, Blue-winged Teal, Cinnamon Teal, and Northern Shoveler hybridize rarely but regularly.

**Date and Location Seen:** _____

Male

Female

**Description:** 46 cm, wingspan 74 cm. Fairly small dabbling duck with **very large spoon-shaped bill**, green speculum, orange legs, **powder-blue forewing patch visible in flight**. MALE: White breast, **rust-brown belly, sides**; iridescent green head, yellow eye, black bill. Dull as female in summer. FEMALE: Mottled brown with dark eye, orangish bill.

**Similar Species:** Bill size, shape distinctive.

**Seasonal Abundance:** Common winter, fairly common summer resident in region; numbers augmented when migrants arrive in late summer. Ranges across northern temperate zone of Old, New Worlds, winters to tropics.

**Where to Find:** Widespread in lowlands, often abundant in sewage lagoons.

**Habitat:** Ponds, lakes, marshes, estuaries, bays, flooded fields.

**Diet and Behaviour:** Feeds while swimming, often in flocks in tight, circling masses. Forages by sweeping bill from side to side to skim, filter at surface for plant, animal matter, seldom upending. May mix with other ducks, but tends to flock with its own species. Courting, pair formation begin late winter; male attains breeding plumage later than other dabblers.

**Voice:** Male gives low calls during courtship; female quacks hoarsely.

**Did you know?** Shovelers' filter-feeding is facilitated by lamellae—transverse ridges inside the edges of the upper and lower bill that act as sieves, trapping food particles.

**Date and Location Seen:** _____

Male

Female

**Description:** 51 cm (male 66 cm with tail), wingspan 84 cm. **Slender**, long-necked dabbling duck with long, thin bill, **green speculum** bordered with buff at front, white at rear. MALE: Greyish with brown head, long, needle-like tail, **white on breast extending in thin line up side of neck**; dull as female in summer. FEMALE: Mottled greyish-brown with short, pointed tail, **dark grey bill**.

**Similar Species:** In female-type plumage, slender shape, dark bill separate pintail from other dabblers.

**Seasonal Abundance:** Common winter resident in region, rare breeder. Highly migratory with transients arriving by August, departing by May. Breeds from Arctic to middle latitudes in North America, Eurasia; winters to tropics.

**Where to Find:** Lowlands; abundant on Boundary Bay, Fraser Delta.

**Habitat:** Ponds, marshes, estuaries, shallow lakes, flooded fields.

**Diet and Behaviour:** Mostly dabbles in shallow water but may walk on land, foraging. Diet mainly plant material including waste grain, also takes insects, aquatic organisms. Gathers in large or small groups, often with other ducks. Courting, pair formation begin in winter.

**Voice:** Fairly vocal, male with fluty *toop toop*, also high buzzy calls; female quacks.

**Did you know?** Northern Pintail is the most abundant duck in the Pacific flyway. The North American population has been estimated at 6 million.

**Date and Location Seen:** _____

Male

Female

**Description:** 33 cm, wingspan 58 cm. **Small** dabbling duck with **short, dark bill, green speculum**. MALE: Greyish with chestnut-and-green head, yellow undertail, **white vertical bar on side**; dull as female in summer. FEMALE: Mottled brown with dark line through eye.

**Similar Species:** Smaller, more compact, shorter-billed than other dabblers; female eye-line more pronounced.

**Seasonal Abundance:** Common winter resident in region, rare breeder. Highly migratory with transients arriving by August, departing by May. Breeds from Arctic to middle latitudes in North America, Eurasia; winters to tropics.

**Where to Find:** Mostly lowlands, rarely in mountains.

**Habitat:** Ponds, marshes, estuaries, bays, shallow lakes, flooded fields.

**Diet and Behaviour:** Forages by dabbling in shallow water or walking on wet mud, filtering water for plant materials, small aquatic organisms. Gathers in large or small groups, often with other ducks. Flocks fly swiftly in tight units, leaving water quickly, apparently with little effort. Courting, pair formation begin in winter.

**Voice:** Male highly vocal with ringing *peep*; female gives weak, nasal quack.

**Did you know?** The Eurasian race, called Common Teal and sometimes considered a separate species, is a rare winter visitor to southwestern British Columbia. It is recognized by the horizontal instead of vertical white bar on the side.

**Date and Location Seen:** _____

Redhead Male

Male

Female

**Description:** 53 cm, wingspan 74 cm. Sleek, elegant, long-necked diving duck with **sloping forehead, long, dark bill**, plain greyish wings. MALE: Black at both ends with **whitish back, sides. Head, neck chestnut-reddish**; eye red. FEMALE: Browner overall, lacks red head, eye.

**Similar Species:** Distinctive head shape, plumage separate Canvasback from scaups (page 59). Male **Redhead** (see inset; rare in region) distinguished by **shape, pattern of head, bill, greyer back**.

**Seasonal Abundance:** Fairly common but local winter resident, arrives by October, most depart by April. Breeds in western North America from central Alaska to South Dakota, winters east to New England, south to Mexico.

**Where to Find:** Throughout lowlands, e.g., Lost Lagoon in Stanley Park, Fraser Delta (especially Iona Island), Esquimalt Lagoon.

**Habitat:** Lakes, estuaries, coastal bays, sewage ponds, marshes.

**Diet and Behaviour:** Dives, mostly in shallow water, primarily for plant materials; may also dabble, take aquatic insects. Sociable; gathers in flocks, often with other ducks. Courts less on wintering grounds than other ducks, as most pair formation occurs later in spring on migration.

**Voice:** Female grunts, male cooing sounds seldom heard in region.

**Did you know?** The Canvasback's Latin species name, *valisineria*, refers to wild celery—an important food item in the eastern and southern United States.

**Date and Location Seen:** _____

Male

Female

**Description:** 43 cm, wingspan 61 cm. Short-necked diving duck with **peaked head, pale ring near tip of grey bill**, greyish wings in flight. MALE: Purplish iridescent head, **black back**, breast; **vertical white mark on grey side** in front of wing. FEMALE: Brownish with **white eye-ring**, diffuse pale facial area near bill.

**Similar Species:** Lesser Scaup (page 59) head less peaked, no ring on bill, male with grey back, female with bold white face patch at bill base.

**Seasonal Abundance:** Common winter resident in region, arrives by September, most depart by May; rare summer resident. Nests northern North America from western Alaska to Labrador, winters to Central America, Caribbean.

**Where to Find:** Mostly lowlands; Elk Lake, Victoria, has large wintering population.

**Habitat:** Ponds, lakes, sewage lagoons, marshes, coastal bays, slow rivers. Prefers fresh water.

**Diet and Behaviour:** Mostly dives, but may also dabble in fairly shallow water. Diet aquatic plants, insects. Sociable. Flocks may be large or small, single-species or mixed with other divers on large water bodies; also flocks with dabblers on small ponds.

**Voice:** Male whistles, female growls softly.

**Did you know?** Unlike other diving ducks, Ring-necked Ducks are able to spring directly off the water into flight, enabling them to use small ponds surrounded by trees.

**Date and Location Seen:** _____

Greater Scaup
Female

Greater Scaup
Male

Lesser Scaup
Male

**Description:** 46 cm / 43 cm, wingspan 71 cm / 66 cm. Short-necked diving ducks with bluish-grey bill, **white wing stripe** visible in flight. MALES: **Blackish on both ends, whitish in middle**, head darkly iridescent. FEMALES: Brownish with **white facial patch at bill base**. GREATER: **Head round**, neck thicker, bill wider, male's head glosses greenish. LESSER: **Peaked crown**, neck thinner, bill smaller, **wing stripe extends only halfway to wingtip**, male's head glosses purplish.

**Similar Species:** Ring-necked Duck (page 57) head more peaked, ring on bill; male with black back, vertical white mark on side.

**Seasonal Abundance:** Common winter residents in region. GREATER: Arrives by October, departs in May. Breeds around world in boreal forest, winters to temperate zone. LESSER: Arrives by October, most depart by April; rare breeder at marshy sewage ponds. Breeds Alaska to Colorado, especially in prairie marshes; winters south as far as Colombia.

**Where to Find:** Mostly lowlands. Both species easily seen, compared at Lost Lagoon, Vancouver.

**Habitat:** Lakes, ponds, bays, estuaries, rivers. GREATER: Prefers large lakes, saltwater habitats. LESSER: Prefers ponds.

**Diet and Behaviour:** Dive for molluscs, other aquatic animals, plants. Highly gregarious, gathering in tight flocks, often including both scaup species, other ducks.

**Voice:** Grating sounds, deep whistles.

**Did you know?** Hunters refer to both species of scaups as Bluebills.

**Date and Location Seen:** _____

Male

Female

**Description:** 41 cm, wingspan 66 cm. Compact, round-headed diving duck with **steep forehead, stubby bill**. MALE: Darkly coloured, mostly **slate-blue with rusty sides, bold white marks** on head, sides, back; dull as female in summer. FEMALE: Brown with white belly, white spot on cheek, another near bill base.

**Similar Species:** Female scoters (pages 63–67) much heavier with larger bills, sloping foreheads; female Bufflehead (page 71) smaller with white wing patch, only one face patch.

**Seasonal Abundance:** Fairly common coastal resident in region, less so in spring when breeding in mountains where uncommon. Breeds in eastern, western North America, Iceland, eastern Asia; winters coastally to temperate zone.

**Where to Find:** Rocky saltwater shorelines; especially common along eastern Vancouver Island. Standard sites include Stanley Park in Vancouver, Ambleside Park in West Vancouver, Clover Point in Victoria. Breeders rarely observed.

**Habitat:** Rocky coastline including bays, exposed locations; breeds on mountain streams.

**Diet and Behaviour:** Forages mostly by diving for molluscs, marine organisms, insects; may also dabble at surface. Gregarious. Courtship begins in winter, pairs form in spring, move up rivers to nest.

**Voice:** Male has piercing whistle, female nasal quacks.

**Did you know?** Female Harlequin Ducks may share in the care of mixed broods.

**Date and Location Seen:** _____

**Male**

**Female**

**Description:** 51 cm, wingspan 76 cm. **Stocky** diving duck with broad, **bulging bill, sloping forehead**, white eye. MALE: All-black with fleshy **orange-yellow-white bill, white patches on forehead, back of neck**, side of bill. FEMALE: Brownish-grey with whitish patches near bill base, on cheek. JUVENILE: Duller than adult, with pale belly, dark eye.

**Similar Species:** Black Scoter (page 67) female has entire lower face whitish, male without white on head, although immature Surf Scoter may also lack this. White-winged Scoter (page 65) has white speculum. Bill shape distinguishes from other ducks in region.

**Seasonal Abundance:** Common winter resident in region, most arrive by August, depart in May. A few non-breeders remain in summer. Nests in far north (western Alaska to Labrador), winters coastally to Baja California, Georgia.

**Where to Find:** Widespread along coast, often over mussel beds.

**Habitat:** Coastal bays, estuaries, exposed surf, rarely fresh water.

**Diet and Behaviour:** Forages by diving, almost exclusively for molluscs while in winter quarters, also other aquatic organisms, plant material. Dives by jumping forward with partially opened wings. Gregarious, often flocking with other scoter species.

**Voice:** Male whistles, female utters croaking grunts.

**Did you know?** During spring migration, huge flocks of Surf Scoters congregate at herring spawn sites along the British Columbia coast. One of these flocks involved an estimated 300,000 birds.

**Date and Location Seen:** _____

Female

Male

**Description:** 56 cm, wingspan 84 cm. **Large** diving duck, **white speculum** visible while flying, diving but may be obscured when at rest. MALE: All-black with white eye, small **white mark behind eye, reddish bill** with small black knob at base. FEMALE: Brownish-grey with dark eye, whitish facial patches. JUVENILE: Duller than adult, with pale belly.

**Similar Species:** Other scoters (pages 63, 67) smaller, lack white speculum; Surf Scoter has different bill shape. Pigeon Guillemot (page 199) smaller with weak flight, white patch at front of wing.

**Seasonal Abundance:** Common winter resident in region (decreasing in recent years), most arrive by October, depart in May. A few non-breeders remain in summer. Nests in western Canada, Alaska, Eurasia, winters to temperate zone.

**Where to Find:** Generally less abundant than Surf Scoter but still common, widespread.

**Habitat:** Coastal bays, estuaries, rarely fresh water (mostly in migration).

**Diet and Behaviour:** Dives with partially opened wings for molluscs, small fish, other marine organisms, plant material. Gregarious, often flocking with other scoters; pairs form on winter quarters. Appears heavy in flight. Flocks move in long, wavering lines low over water.

**Voice:** Male whistles; female grunts seldom heard.

**Did you know?** The Eurasian race, sometimes considered a separate species, is called Velvet Scoter.

**Date and Location Seen:** _____

Male

Female

**Description:** 48 cm, wingspan 71 cm. **Stocky** diving duck with **fairly small black bill**. MALE: All-black with fleshy **yellowish-orange knob** at bill base. FEMALE: Brownish-grey with **entire lower face, cheek whitish-grey**. JUVENILE: Similar to female, with pale belly.

**Similar Species:** Bill much smaller, held more horizontal than other scoters (pages 63–65). Female smaller with more extensive pale cheek patch (other female scoters have two smaller, whitish face patches). White-winged has white speculum. Ruddy Duck (page 81) smaller with large, broad bill, longer tail.

**Seasonal Abundance:** Mostly uncommon (locally fairly common) winter resident in region, arrives by November, departs by April. Breeds on tundra, winters coastally in temperate zone of northern hemisphere. North American race sometimes treated as separate species from Eurasian races.

**Where to Find:** Inland marine waters, e.g., Point Grey in Vancouver, Little Qualicum estuary, Island View Beach in Saanich.

**Habitat:** Coastal waters with rocky or gravelly bottoms.

**Diet and Behaviour:** Takes primarily molluscs obtained by diving; also other marine organisms, insects, plant material. Gregarious, flocking with other scoters, often in fairly tight groups. Courtship progresses throughout winter to spring.

**Voice:** More vocal than other scoters: grunts, whistles.

**Did you know?** Black is the least common scoter in the region. Some 250,000 breed in Alaska, yet fewer than 5,000 winter on the Pacific Coast south of Anchorage.

**Date and Location Seen:** _____

**Male Non-breeding**

**Female Non-breeding**

**Description:** 41 cm (male 53 cm with tail), wingspan 69 cm. Short-necked, white-bellied, **stubby-billed** diving duck, short **blackish wings**. Plumage unusually variable due to three annual adult moults. MALE: Elegant, usually with **long, pointed tail**; bill dark with pink band. Breeding (spring) plumage mostly black with white face, non-breeding (winter) **mostly white** with black back, breast, neck patch. FEMALE: Bill bluish-green; dark overall, face whitish in non-breeding plumage.

**Similar Species:** In flight, combination of dark wings, whitish body unique among ducks. Markings different from Northern Pintail (page 51), neck longer than alcids (pages 197–203, 401).

**Seasonal Abundance:** Fairly common but local winter resident in region, arrives mid-October, departs by May. Breeds on Arctic tundra in Old, New Worlds, winters to temperate zone.

**Where to Find:** Marine waters. Look for it especially at White Rock, in Victoria vicinity, up east coast of Vancouver Island.

**Habitat:** Coastal waters, extremely rarely on fresh water in region.

**Diet and Behaviour:** Dives for molluscs, other marine organisms, some plant material. Sociable, although flocks in region smaller than in most of range.

**Voice:** Male very vocal with loud yodelling when spring courtship begins in winter quarters. Female gives soft grunts.

**Did you know?** Accomplished divers, Long-tailed Ducks have been recorded at depths exceeding 60 metres.

**Date and Location Seen:** _____

**Male**

**Female**

**Description:** 33 cm, wingspan 51 cm. **Small**, plump diving duck, with small grey bill, white belly, white wing patches easily visible in flight. MALE: Mostly white with dark back, iridescent blackish, **puffy head with white patch at back**. FEMALE: Dull greyish with small, **oval white cheek patch**, smaller wing patches than male.

**Similar Species:** Goldeneyes (page 73) larger, white patch of male below rather than behind eye. Hooded Merganser (page 75) male has rusty sides with black-and-white bars. Ruddy Duck (page 81) has larger bill, cheek patch.

**Seasonal Abundance:** Common winter resident in region. Most arrive October, depart by May; rare in summer. Nests in interior from central Alaska to Quebec, winters on both coasts from Aleutians, Maritimes south to Mexico.

**Where to Find:** Throughout lowlands.

**Habitat:** Found on freshwater, saltwater bodies of all sizes, even deeply flooded fields.

**Diet and Behaviour:** Dives for insects, other aquatic organisms, plant materials. Usually in small groups, but large concentrations occur at favourable sites. Patters on surface with rapid wingbeats before flying.

**Voice:** Fairly quiet in winter quarters but soft, growling whistles, grunts occasionally given.

**Did you know?** *Bucephala*—the scientific name of the genus—comes from a Greek word meaning ox-headed. The species' common name evokes the high, domed forehead of the American bison (buffalo).

## Date and Location Seen: _____

Common Goldeneye
Male

Common Goldeneye
Female

Barrow's Goldeneye
Male

Barrow's Goldeneye
Female

**Description:** 46 cm, wingspan 69 cm. Plump, short-necked, with short bill, **puffy head, white wing patch**. MALES: White with black-and-white back, dark iridescent head, white patch below eye. FEMALES: Greyish with brown head. COMMON: Head peaked in middle, male's **green with round patch**; less black on back. BARROW'S: Head peaked at front, **steep forehead**, bill smaller. Male's **head purplish, patch crescent-shaped**; less white on back.

**Similar Species:** Bufflehead (page 71) smaller, male's head patch behind rather than below eye.

**Seasonal Abundance:** Fairly common winter residents in region. COMMON: Arrives by November, departs by April, rarely present in summer. Breeds across northern North America, Eurasia, winters to temperate zone. BARROW'S: Arrives in lowlands by October, departs by April; uncommon breeder in mainland mountains. Breeds Alaska to Wyoming, also northeastern Canada, Iceland; winters down both coasts in temperate zone.

**Where to Find:** Lowlands. BARROW'S: Summer in mountains.

**Habitat:** COMMON: Coastal bays, rivers, lakes, sewage ponds. BARROW'S: Mostly marine waters, often near dock pilings, rocky shores with mussel beds; also large rivers.

**Diet and Behaviour:** Dive for aquatic animals, plants; flock outside nesting season. Nest in tree cavities on forested mountain lakes.

**Voice:** Soft grunts.

**Did you know?** Most of the world's Barrow's Goldeneyes nest in British Columbia.

**Date and Location Seen:** _____

Male

Female

**Description:** 41 cm, wingspan 58 cm. Small, **long-tailed** duck with thin, **sawtoothed bill**, conspicuous **puffy crest**, white belly. Small white wing patches visible in flight. MALE: Striking; mostly blackish above including bill, with fan-shaped white crest, rusty sides, black-and-white side bars, ornamental back plumes; dull as female in late summer. FEMALE: Brownish-grey with yellowish-edged bill.

**Similar Species:** Other mergansers (pages 77–79) larger, with reddish bills. Bufflehead (page 71) female smaller with small cheek patch; male has white sides.

**Seasonal Abundance:** Fairly common resident in region, less common in summer. Ranges from southeastern Alaska to Oregon, also Great Lakes to New Brunswick; winters to California, southeastern U.S.

**Where to Find:** Mostly lowlands. Large numbers on Elk Lake, Victoria.

**Habitat:** Breeds at wooded freshwater ponds, sloughs, sluggish creeks with emergent vegetation. Migrants, wintering groups also use estuaries, sewage ponds.

**Diet and Behaviour:** Forages visually by diving, swimming underwater for fish, aquatic insects, other organisms. Usually in small groups, but may concentrate at favourable sites in fall. Often allows close approach, then patters along surface with rapid wingbeats, flies off. Nests in tree cavities, also nest boxes.

**Voice:** Fairly vocal with soft croaks.

**Did you know?** Hooded Mergansers occasionally hybridize with other cavity-nesting ducks, especially goldeneyes.

**Date and Location Seen:** _____

Male

Female

**Description:** 61 cm, wingspan 86 cm. **Robust**, white-bellied diving duck, with thin, **reddish sawtoothed bill, shaggy crest**. Large white wing patches visible in flight. MALE: Body mostly white with dark green head, dark back; dull as female in late summer. FEMALE: Grey with brown head, white chin.

**Similar Species:** Red-breasted Merganser (page 79) female very similar but less bulky, with neither distinct white throat nor abrupt line between light grey body, brown head; bill thinner at base. Hooded Merganser (page 75) much smaller, bill not reddish.

**Seasonal Abundance:** Common resident in region. Ranges across forested areas of northern hemisphere to southern edge of temperate zone.

**Where to Find:** Throughout region, sea level to mountain passes.

**Habitat:** Principally forested areas with fresh, clear water (rivers, lakes), but also coastal bays; often in brackish river mouths.

**Diet and Behaviour:** Forages visually by diving, swimming underwater, mostly for fish; young eat aquatic insects. Concentrates in large flocks from late summer to early winter in rivers, coastal estuaries, where pair formation begins. Nests near water in tree cavities, mostly along major rivers, but also near clear lakes; may be loosely colonial.

**Voice:** Hoarse croaking notes.

**Did you know?** In the Old World this species is called Goosander.

**Date and Location Seen:** _____

Male

Female

**Description:** 56 cm, wingspan 76 cm. **Slim**, long-necked, white-bellied diving duck with long, thin, **reddish sawtoothed bill**, conspicuous **shaggy crest**. Large **white wing patches** visible in flight. MALE: Elegant with green head, white neck-ring, dark back, grey sides; dull as female in late summer. FEMALE: Grey with brown head.

**Similar Species:** Common Merganser (page 77) female very similar but bulkier, with distinct white throat, abrupt line between light grey body, brown head; bill thicker at base. Hooded Merganser (page 75) smaller, bill not reddish.

**Seasonal Abundance:** Common winter resident in region, rare in summer. Most arrive October, depart by April. Breeds across northern North America, Eurasia to treeline, winters coastally to subtropics.

**Where to Find:** Widespread throughout region on sheltered marine waters, e.g., off Fraser Delta, in Boundary Bay.

**Habitat:** Coastal bays, estuaries; extremely rare on fresh water in region.

**Diet and Behaviour:** Forages by diving, swimming underwater, mostly for fish. Loose flocks occasionally fish cooperatively by herding schooling fish. Courtship behaviour increases throughout late fall, winter as males attain breeding plumage.

**Voice:** Relatively silent. Females may give harsh, grating squawks.

**Did you know?** One of the fastest-flying ducks, Red-breasted Mergansers have been clocked at 160 kilometres per hour.

**Date and Location Seen:** _____

Male Breeding

Female

**Description:** 38 cm, wingspan 48 cm. Compact, **large-headed, broad-billed** diving duck with **long, stiff tail** often cocked upward. MALE: In breeding plumage (spring–summer) reddish-brown with black head, neck, **white cheek, powder-blue bill**; dull brown in fall–winter (retains black cap, white cheek). FEMALE: Brownish, **light cheek crossed by dark line**.

**Similar Species:** Female Bufflehead (page 71) with bill, cheek patch smaller.

**Seasonal Abundance:** Locally common winter resident in region, uncommon breeder. Nests western North America; winters in southern U.S., along both coasts, south through Mexico. Also resident western South America.

**Where to Find:** Fresh water, protected coastal sites.

**Habitat:** Lowland ponds, lakes, sewage lagoons, bays. Breeds on fresh water with marshy edge.

**Diet and Behaviour:** Dives, feeds mostly on aquatic plants, some insects. Sits low in water when active but sleeps buoyantly on surface. Often in large groups when not nesting. Patters along water, flapping short wings rapidly to take flight; clumsy on land. Male courtship unique—raises tail to expose white underneath, pumps head rapidly, followed by boisterous rushes across water.

**Voice:** Courting male produces stuttering series of ticks while pumping bill against inflated throat; female gives nasal call in defence of young.

**Did you know?** Unlike other ducks, male Ruddies keep their dull "eclipse" plumage through the fall and winter.

**Date and Location Seen:** _____

Male

Female

# RING-NECKED PHEASANT
### *Phasianus colchicus*

**Description:** 53 cm (male 76 cm with tail), wingspan 79 cm. Large, **chicken-like** bird with **long tail**. Mostly mottled shades of brown. MALE: More colourful—orangish flanks, grey rump, **white neck-ring, iridescent green head, red skin on face**.

**Similar Species:** Other large "chickens" in region shorter-tailed, males drab; usually found in forests. Ruffed Grouse (page 85) smaller; Blue Grouse (page 387) greyish with grey-tipped tail.

**Seasonal Abundance:** Uncommon year-round resident in region. Native to Asia, widely introduced as game bird elsewhere.

**Where to Find:** Rural, semi-rural lowlands on Lower Mainland, eastern Vancouver Island. Released or escaped pen-raised birds augment populations in some areas.

**Habitat:** Open fields, brush patches, woodland edges, lightly developed residential areas, large parks.

**Diet and Behaviour:** Forages on ground, also in brush, trees. Opportunistic. Consumes agricultural grains, weed seeds, roots, fruits, nuts, leaves, insects (adults, larvae), earthworms, snails. Prefers to walk or run but strong flyer when flushed. Takes off explosively on whirring wings. Young follow female, forage for themselves upon hatching. May form flocks in winter.

**Voice:** Male crowing, alarm call loud, grating *krrok ook*; also softer clucking sounds (both sexes).

**Did you know?** Pheasants were first introduced to southwestern British Columbia in 1882 when 25 were released at Victoria. Introductions on the mainland began in 1890. Local populations have declined by about 90 percent in the last 30 years.

**Date and Location Seen:** _____

**Description:** 46 cm, wingspan 56 cm. Variably brownish, cryptically patterned, **chicken-like** bird with barred flanks, small crest (sometimes flattened). Reddish to greyish **tail with black band near tip**.

**Similar Species:** Ring-necked Pheasant (page 83) much larger, long-tailed; usually found in open country. Blue Grouse (page 387) somewhat larger, tail dark with grey tip, male uniformly darker; inhabits coniferous forests.

**Seasonal Abundance:** Fairly common year-round resident in region. Ranges across continent's northern forest zones.

**Where to Find:** Widespread throughout wooded regions but secretive; usually detected by male's drumming or when female wanders into view with brood.

**Habitat:** Low to mid-elevation deciduous or mixed forests with developed understory, ground layer, often along stream corridors.

**Diet and Behaviour:** Leaves, fruits, other plant materials; buds important in winter. Chicks feed themselves upon hatching, mostly small invertebrates at first—can fly within week. Solitary in breeding season, may form small, loose winter flocks. Males "drum" from log, other ground perches, mostly in spring.

**Voice:** Unremarkable. Female sometimes makes clucking, cooing sounds.

**Did you know?** Drumming is an accelerating series of sonic booms as air rushes to fill the vacuum produced by the male's wing movements. Young birds require long practice to master the technique.

**Date and Location Seen:** _____

Male

Female

**Description:** 25 cm, wingspan 36 cm. Elegant little gamefowl with **forward-drooping topknot. Greyish overall, scaled belly**, brown sides with lighter barring. MALE: Chestnut patch on belly, **white eyebrow, black throat outlined in white**, larger topknot.

**Similar Species:** Smaller than pheasant (page 83), grouse (pages 85, 387). No other quails occur regularly in region.

**Seasonal Abundance:** Fairly common but local resident; absent from mainland. Native along Pacific Coast from southern Oregon through Baja California; introduced north to Washington, southern British Columbia.

**Where to Find:** Limited to Saltspring Island, Pender Islands, lowlands of southeastern Vancouver Island north to Comox.

**Habitat:** Open, grassy woodlands, farmland, suburban gardens. Needs mix of dense shrubbery for cover, open ground for foraging.

**Diet and Behaviour:** Eats mostly plant material (seeds, leaves, etc.), some invertebrates. Sociable. Coveys disband for breeding but stay within winter territory. Prolific—two broods some years, up to 20 eggs (or more) per clutch.

**Voice:** Loud *chi ca go* assembly call; variety of other contact, alarm, advertising calls.

**Did you know?** Coveys post male sentries to warn of danger. Look for them on fence posts or other prominent perches.

**Date and Location Seen:** _____

Non-breeding

Breeding

**Description:** 64 cm, wingspan 91 cm. Smallest loon. **Thin bill** appears slightly upcurved, **usually held slightly upward**. NON-BREEDING: **Pale** with white on face, throat, neck; **grey back** speckled with white. BREEDING: **Dark back**, grey head, neck, **red throat**.

**Similar Species:** Common Loon (page 93) larger, darker, with thicker bill; less white on face, neck in non-breeding plumage. Pacific Loon (page 91) about same size with straight bill usually held level, unmarked dark back.

**Seasonal Abundance:** Fairly common winter resident in region, arrives September, departs by May; some nest locally on lakes near coast. Breeds in Canada, Alaska, Eurasia, winters along coasts in temperate zone.

**Where to Find:** Widespread in winter along coastlines; especially common at mouth of Fraser River. Breeds on Vancouver Island, central mainland.

**Habitat:** Outside breeding season, mostly shallow, protected saltwater bays, river mouths. Freshwater lakes for nesting, rarely also in winter.

**Diet and Behaviour:** Mainly small fish obtained by diving. Usually feeds singly or in small flocks, sometimes in large flocks at prey concentrations.

**Voice:** Wailing, barking on breeding grounds; usually silent in winter.

**Did you know?** Red-throated Loon is the only loon that can take flight from land rather than running across the water.

**Date and Location Seen:** _____

Non-breeding

Breeding

# PACIFIC LOON
## *Gavia pacifica*

**Description:** 66 cm, wingspan 91 cm. Smooth, **rounded head; slender bill** held horizontally. NON-BREEDING: **Dark back**, dark around eye, clean white throat, breast. **Dark back of neck sharply separated from white front** of neck; thin, dark chin strap often visible. BREEDING: **Silver-grey crown, nape**, black back with white checkering. **Dark throat patch**, vertical white stripes on sides of neck.

**Similar Species:** Red-throated Loon (page 89) holds bill slightly upward; paler back, more white on neck, face; red throat patch in breeding plumage. Common Loon (page 93) larger with thicker bill, steep forehead; in non-breeding plumage, lacks clean separation between throat, back of neck; has white around eye.

**Seasonal Abundance:** Fairly common resident in region, September–May. Breeds on Subarctic/Arctic lakes in Canada, Alaska, northeastern Siberia, winters farther south along coast on both sides of Pacific.

**Where to Find:** Saltwater habitats throughout region, but locally abundant at sites with rich upwelling currents such as Active Pass, Porlier Pass, Discovery Passage; also large numbers at herring spawn events.

**Habitat:** Open salt water; prefers deeper waters than other loons.

**Diet and Behaviour:** Dives for small fish. Often seen in large, concentrated flocks where food supply abundant.

**Voice:** Calls mainly on breeding grounds.

**Did you know?** Pacific Loons migrate in flocks, more so than other loons.

**Date and Location Seen:** _____

Non-breeding

Breeding

**Description:** 81 cm, wingspan 117 cm. **Large** loon with **thick bill**, steep forehead. NON-BREEDING: White throat, **pale around eye**; back dark with lighter mottling. **Traces of white collar extending back on upper neck**, dark collar extending forward on lower neck. BREEDING: **Head, bill black; black collar**, dark back checkered white.

**Similar Species:** Yellow-billed Loon (not shown; rare in region) similar but slightly larger with larger, yellowish bill (Common has dark ridge on top in non-breeding plumage). Red-throated Loon (page 89) more finely built; thin bill held slightly upward. Pacific Loon (page 91) smaller; in non-breeding plumage, sharp contrast between white throat, dark back of neck.

**Seasonal Abundance:** Common winter resident in region; uncommon, local breeder. Breeds across northern North America to Iceland, winters south along coasts.

**Where to Find:** In winter, anywhere on salt water (a few non-breeders also in summer). Nests on lakes, e.g., Lightning Lake in Manning Park.

**Habitat:** Winters on open salt water (occasionally freshwater lakes).

**Diet and Behaviour:** Small fish caught, swallowed underwater. Usually forages singly.

**Voice:** Distinctive loud yodelling, mostly during breeding season but also sometimes in flight during migration.

**Did you know?** Nesting Common Loons require near-pristine conditions and are sensitive to human disturbance.

**Date and Location Seen:** _____

Breeding

Non-breeding

**Description:** 33 cm, wingspan 41 cm. **Brownish, short-necked, stocky** grebe with **thick, short, pale bill, white undertail**. BREEDING: Forehead, throat black, bill white with black ring. Chicks show extensive head streaking.

**Similar Species:** Horned Grebe (page 97) has longer, thinner bill; head, neck contrasting black-and-white in non-breeding plumage. Red-necked Grebe (page 99) larger, longer-billed.

**Seasonal Abundance:** Fairly common breeder in region, becomes common in winter as birds arrive from interior. Ranges from Prairie provinces south to Central, South America, vacating areas where lakes freeze in winter.

**Where to Find:** Throughout lowlands; also on higher-elevation lakes in migration. Nests in city parks with emergent vegetation—for example, Jericho Park in Vancouver, Burnaby Lake Regional Park.

**Habitat:** Freshwater marshes, lakes, ponds, with smaller numbers on protected salt water in winter.

**Diet and Behaviour:** Small fish, aquatic insects, crustaceans taken underwater. To submerge, may dive headfirst or simply allow itself to sink; often resurfaces some distance away. Rarely seen in flocks.

**Voice:** In breeding season, loud *cuck cuck cuck, cow cow cow, cowah cowah*.

**Did you know?** Pied-billed Grebe is the most widespread grebe in North America and in the region.

**Date and Location Seen:** _____

**Eared Grebe
Non-breeding**

**Non-breeding**

**Breeding**

**Description:** 36 cm, wingspan 46 cm. Relatively flat head, red eye, straight bill with light tip. Rides low in water. NON-BREEDING: Back, back of neck, crown dark grey; **front of neck, throat, cheeks whitish**. BREEDING: Back greyish, **neck reddish, head black with golden "horns" from eye to back of head**.

**Similar Species: Eared Grebe** (see inset; rare in region in migration, winter) slighter, bill thinner; thin-necked, rides high in water. In non-breeding plumage, **cheek dark, top of head peaks above eye**. Neck blackish in breeding plumage. Pied-billed Grebe (page 95) overall brownish with thick bill. Western Grebe (page 101) larger with longer neck, bill.

**Seasonal Abundance:** Common winter resident in region, late August–April. Breeds on interior lakes, marshes of northern North America, Eurasia; winters southward.

**Where to Find:** Widespread in lowlands.

**Habitat:** Saltwater bays, inlets, channels; smaller numbers on large freshwater lakes, slow-moving rivers.

**Diet and Behaviour:** In winter, feeds mostly on small fish obtained by diving.

**Voice:** Mostly silent in winter; high, thin notes occasionally heard.

**Did you know?** Horned Grebes can stay submerged up to three minutes and swim 150 metres below the surface on one dive.

**Date and Location Seen:** _____

Non-breeding

Breeding

**Description:** 51 cm, wingspan 61 cm. Large, grey-brown grebe with dark eye, flat, wedge-shaped head, **thick neck**, tapered **yellowish bill**. NON-BREEDING: Back, crown dark; **cheek, neck dingy grey, light ear patch**. BREEDING: Black crown, **reddish-brown neck**, pale grey cheeks, throat.

**Similar Species:** More than twice as heavy as Horned Grebe (page 97), Pied-billed Grebe (page 95). Horned has shorter neck, thinner bill, red eye. Pied-billed brown overall with thick, stubby bill. Larger Western Grebe (page 101) clean grey-and-white with longer, thinner neck, bill.

**Seasonal Abundance:** Common winter resident throughout region; begins returning late July, most depart March. Breeding range northern North America, Eurasia; winters south along coasts.

**Where to Find:** Widespread. Numerous off Fraser Delta, especially in Boundary Bay.

**Habitat:** Favours deep saltwater sites—open waters, large bays, inlets; much lower numbers on large lowland lakes.

**Diet and Behaviour:** Dives for small fish.

**Voice:** Not often heard in winter.

**Did you know?** Red-necked Grebes nest on marshy lakes in the British Columbia interior. Like other grebes, they build floating nests and carry their young on their backs.

**Date and Location Seen:** _____

**Description:** 64 cm, wingspan 61 cm. **Long-necked, black-and-white** grebe with **long, thin, dull yellow bill**. Neck white in front, black behind. White throat, cheeks; black cap extends down to include red eye.

**Similar Species:** Clark's Grebe (not shown; rare winter visitor in region) almost identical but lighter-appearing; bill orange-yellow, dark cap may not cover eye. Red-necked Grebe (page 99) has shorter neck, dark eye; in non-breeding plumage, neck grey (not white). Horned Grebe (page 97) smaller with short neck, smaller dark bill.

**Seasonal Abundance:** Common resident in region, September–May; a few non-breeders present in summer. Nests on lakes in interior western North America (Manitoba to California); winters along coast from southeastern Alaska to northwestern Mexico.

**Where to Find:** Throughout region. Good numbers usually in English Bay, Nanaimo harbour, off Iona Island, Oyster River estuary.

**Habitat:** Sheltered saltwater bays, inlets; also large freshwater lakes.

**Diet and Behaviour:** Eats mostly fish, obtained by diving. Often forms large flocks in winter.

**Voice:** Loud, high, two-note *crick creek* call, given all year.

**Did you know?** Wintering populations of Western Grebe in the region have declined dramatically over the past decade.

**Date and Location Seen:** _____

**Non-breeding**

**Description:** 89 cm, wingspan 122 cm. **All-dark with buffy chin.** In flight, holds thick neck nearly straight, shows **short tail**. BREEDING: **Blue throat pouch** (visible at close range), fine white feathers on head, neck, back. IMMATURE: Plain dark brown with tan breast.

**Similar Species:** Pelagic Cormorant (page 107) has thinner neck, head, bill; longer tail; white flank patch during breeding season. Double-crested Cormorant (page 105) has orange at lower base of bill; longer wings, tail; flies with noticeable crook in neck.

**Seasonal Abundance:** Fairly common for most of year in southern part of region, less common in northern part. Rare breeder on islets off southwestern Vancouver Island, scarce or absent elsewhere in region during nesting season. Breeds colonially along coast from southwestern British Columbia to Baja California.

**Where to Find:** Widespread along coast, large flocks gather at sites with strong tidal currents such as Active Pass between Mayne, Galiano islands.

**Habitat:** Exclusively saltwater; rarely even flies over land.

**Diet and Behaviour:** Dives for fish, crabs, shrimp. Gregarious. Flies in long lines low over water.

**Voice:** Usually silent except at nest.

**Did you know?** A few Brandt's Cormorants nest on the west coast of Vancouver Island, but most nest farther south. Many southern breeders disperse northward to winter on the fish-rich British Columbia coast.

**Date and Location Seen:** _____

**Non-breeding**

**Immature**

# DOUBLE-CRESTED CORMORANT
## *Phalacrocorax auritus*

**Description:** 81 cm, wingspan 132 cm. **All-dark** with long tail, thick neck, **yellow-orange facial skin**, throat pouch. In flight, **holds thick neck with pronounced crook**. BREEDING: **White tufts behind eye**. IMMATURE: Brown with paler breast, neck.

**Similar Species:** Brandt's (page 103), Pelagic (page 107) Cormorants have shorter wings, fly with neck held straighter. Pelagic's bill, head, neck much thinner. In breeding plumage, Pelagic has white flank patch, red skin on face. Brandt's has buffy chin in all plumages.

**Seasonal Abundance:** Common resident in region; numbers increase in winter. Nests along both coasts of North America, also interior of continent. Winters along coasts south to Gulf of California, Gulf of Mexico.

**Where to Find:** Throughout lowlands. Breeds on small islands in southern Strait of Georgia.

**Habitat:** Saltwater bays, estuaries, shorelines; freshwater lakes, ponds, rivers, marshes. Only local cormorant on fresh water.

**Diet and Behaviour:** Dives for small fish. Sometimes flies high in V-formation like geese. Often flies over land. Swims low in water with head tilted slightly upward. Often perches with wings outstretched to dry them.

**Voice:** Quiet away from breeding grounds.

**Did you know?** Double-crested Cormorant breeding populations in the Strait of Georgia decreased sharply in the 1990s, due at least in part to nest predation by Bald Eagles.

**Date and Location Seen:** _____

**Breeding**

**Description:** 69 cm, wingspan 99 cm. **Smallest local cormorant**. Dark with greenish sheen (visible in good light). **Slender neck, head, pencil-thin black bill** (like flying snake). BREEDING: **White flank patch, red facial skin**. IMMATURE: Uniformly dark brown.

**Similar Species:** Brandt's Cormorant (page 103) has shorter tail, band of buffy feathers at base of bill. Double-crested Cormorant (page 105) has yellow-orange facial skin, flies with crook in neck. Pelagic Cormorant slimmer overall than either, with much thinner neck, head, bill.

**Seasonal Abundance:** Common breeder, year-round resident in region. Ranges along both sides of North Pacific from Bering Strait to Japan, California.

**Where to Find:** Widespread along coast; at least a few breed on almost every rocky island, coastal bluff.

**Habitat:** Strictly saltwater: piers, pilings, bluffs, rocky shorelines.

**Diet and Behaviour:** Dives deep for fish, crustaceans, other invertebrates. Has been caught in fishermen's nets at depths of 55 metres.

**Voice:** Grunts, croaks, groans on breeding grounds.

**Did you know?** Pelagic Cormorants can leap directly from the water into flight. Other cormorants must run along the surface to gain takeoff speed.

**Date and Location Seen:** _____

American Bittern

Green Heron

**Description:** 71 cm / 43 cm, wingspan 107 cm / 66 cm. Stocky waders, fly with neck pulled in. BITTERN: Larger, **streaked brownish**, black stripe on side of neck, **greenish legs**. Dark, pointed flight feathers contrast with back. HERON: **Small**, dark greenish above, purplish-rufous below, white streaking at breast center, **orangish legs**; immature brown-streaked below.

**Similar Species:** Immature Black-crowned Night-Heron (not shown; rare in region) similar to bittern with rounder, even-coloured wings.

**Seasonal Abundance:** Uncommon residents in region, rare in winter. Range across North America, winter to Central America.

**Where to Find:** Throughout lowlands. BITTERN: Reifel Sanctuary (winter), Pitt Meadows marshes (breeding). HERON: DeBouville Slough (Port Coquitlam). Many other sites for both.

**Habitat:** BITTERN: Large freshwater/brackish open marshes. HERON: Sheltered freshwater sites with overhanging trees.

**Diet and Behaviour:** Secretive, usually solitary. Forage mostly at water, primarily for fish. BITTERN: Hides with neck extended, bill pointing up; nests on ground in marsh. HERON: Nests in trees.

**Voice:** BITTERN: Deep pump-like *boonk ahh soonk*; squawks in alarm. HERON: Loud *kyow*.

**Did you know?** Green Herons are slowly extending their range northward; they first appeared in British Columbia in 1953. American Bitterns are declining across their range.

**Date and Location Seen:** _____

# GREAT BLUE HERON
## *Ardea herodias*

**Description:** 122 cm, wingspan 183 cm. **Long-necked**, long-legged wader with **dagger-like bill**. Mostly bluish-grey above, lighter below, **white face topped with black plumes**. In flight neck usually pulled in, legs trail behind; wings broad, slightly cupped. JUVENILE, NON-BREEDING: Duller; dark forehead.

**Similar Species:** Great Egret (not shown; rare in region) slightly smaller, all-white. Black-crowned Night-Heron (not shown; rare in region) somewhat similar in plumage but considerably smaller with short neck, bill.

**Seasonal Abundance:** Common resident in region. Ranges across North America from southern Alaska to Maritimes, south to northern South America.

**Where to Find:** Throughout region; especially common around Fraser Delta, Tsawwassen ferry jetty, Blackie Spit in Crescent Beach.

**Habitat:** Marshes, ponds, estuaries, agricultural fields, rivers, lakes.

**Diet and Behaviour:** Forages by standing or walking slowly, equally likely in water or fields. Extremely varied diet includes any animal life that can be grasped or speared with bill; rodents important component in region. Nests primarily in colonies in tall dead or dying trees.

**Voice:** Loud croaking, often drawn-out *frahhhnnk*, usually given when flushed.

**Did you know?** Great Blue Herons may be mistaken for Sandhill Cranes (not shown; rare in region) but are not related to the cranes, which never fly with their necks pulled in as herons do.

**Date and Location Seen:** _____

**Description:** 66 cm, wingspan 168 cm. Blackish, long-tailed, with small, bare **red head**; soars on long, fairly broad, two-toned **wings held above horizontal in tipping, unsteady flight**. Appears plump when perched. JUVENILE: Black head.

**Similar Species:** Immature Bald Eagle (page 117), Red-tailed Hawk (page 125) soar with wings held flatter; heads larger, different underwing patterns. Northern Harrier (page 119) similar in flight but tail, wings longer, rump white.

**Seasonal Abundance:** Fairly common but local summer resident in region. Arrives by March, departs by October; a few winter, especially on southern Vancouver Island. Ranges from southern Canada to South America.

**Where to Find:** Throughout region; most common eastern Vancouver Island, Fraser Valley. In September, hundreds circle over Sooke, Metchosin at southern end of Vancouver Island, waiting for favourable winds to cross Juan de Fuca Strait.

**Habitat:** Open areas such as agricultural fields, clear-cuts, in proximity to forested hills.

**Diet and Behaviour:** Soars, searching for dead animals by sight, smell. Seldom flaps, relying on thermals for soaring. Gregarious, usually roosting, migrating, feeding in groups. Reluctantly crosses water bodies in migration.

**Voice:** Grunting, hissing (seldom heard).

**Did you know?** Unlike the vultures of Africa and Eurasia, the Turkey Vulture is not in the hawk and eagle family. Instead it is closely related to the storks.

**Date and Location Seen:** _____

**Description:** 58 cm, wingspan 160 cm. **Blackish above** except for **whitish crown. Mostly white underparts** contrast with **dark mask**, strongly banded wings, tail. Wings long, somewhat angled (gull-like) with dark patch at wrist.

**Similar Species:** Immature Bald Eagle (page 117) in transitional plumage never has all-white underparts, but may show dark mask on white head. Gulls have more pointed wings.

**Seasonal Abundance:** Fairly common summer resident in region, arrives late March, most depart by October but a few linger—very rarely to winter. Ranges worldwide; northern birds winter to southern continents.

**Where to Find:** Throughout region; nests at Maplewood Flats (North Vancouver), Pitt Lake, Elk Lake (Victoria).

**Habitat:** Usually near water including rivers, lakes, estuaries, but migrants may be far from water.

**Diet and Behaviour:** Feeds almost exclusively on live fish, hovering over water, plunging feet-first, sometimes catching prey well below surface. Feet equipped with bumps called spicules that assist talons in holding fish. Pairs raise young on top of broken tree, power tower, platform, building bulky nest, often near human habitation. May be loosely colonial.

**Voice:** Noisy, calling with slurred, shrill whistles.

**Did you know?** This unique species, often classified in a family of its own, is rebounding from severe losses resulting from DDT.

**Date and Location Seen:** _____

First-year

First-year

**Description:** 84 cm, wingspan 208 cm. ADULT: Dark brown with **white head, tail**; feet, eye, huge bill yellow. Soars on **long, broad wings**. FIRST-YEAR: Lacks white head, tail; bill, eye dark. Birds transition to adult plumage, bill, eye colour over four years.

**Similar Species:** Hawks have shorter wings. Golden Eagle (not shown; uncommon in region) has golden feathers on nape, smaller head, bill; immature with white patches at center of wing, base of tail.

**Seasonal Abundance:** Common resident in region, harder to find in early fall when disperses to north. Ranges Alaska to Labrador, south to northern Mexico.

**Where to Find:** Mostly lowlands. Concentrates at herring spawn events, midwinter salmon runs (e.g., Cheakamus, Squamish rivers at Brackendale, Harrison River), also in winter on coastal mud flats.

**Habitat:** Usually near bodies of water—coastline, lakes, rivers.

**Diet and Behaviour:** Feeds mostly on fish when available, including spawned-out salmon in rivers, also water birds, carrion, other prey; steals food from smaller raptors. Pairs return to territories in mid-fall, may work on nests; eggs laid by early March, young fledge by late July.

**Voice:** Far-carrying series of chirping whistles, piercing screams.

**Did you know?** After breeding, many Bald Eagles from all over western North America arrive in British Columbia to feast on spawning salmon. More than 3,000 birds may gather on the Cheakamus River in midwinter.

**Date and Location Seen:** _____

Female

Male

**Description:** 48 cm, wingspan 112 cm. Slim, **long-winged**, with **owl-like face**, long, banded tail, **white rump**. Usually flies with **wings held above horizontal**. MALE: Adult grey (whiter below) with black wingtips. FEMALE: Larger; brown above, streaked below. IMMATURE: Resembles female, but juvenile orangish on breast, lacks streaks.

**Similar Species:** White rump distinctive. Rough-legged Hawk (page 127) has white tail base, not rump. Red-tailed Hawk (page 125) has broader wings. Cooper's Hawk (page 123) smaller, holds wings flatter. Falcons have more pointed wings, swifter flight.

**Seasonal Abundance:** Locally common migrant, winter resident in region, uncommon breeder. Ranges across northern hemisphere, winters to northern tropics. North American population sometimes considered separate species.

**Where to Find:** Lowlands; migrants rarely in mountains, urban areas. Especially common on Fraser Delta, Boundary Bay dykes.

**Habitat:** Marshes, fields, agricultural flats, occasionally clear-cuts.

**Diet and Behaviour:** Courses low, "harries" prey, using vision, hearing to locate movement, then dives to flush, catch small mammals, birds. May hover briefly. Concentrates at productive locations to hunt, roost. Nests on ground.

**Voice:** Calls include whistles, also rapid chatter heard while breeding, occasionally on winter quarters.

**Did you know?** Male Northern Harriers may mate with several females. Courting pairs perform spectacular roller-coaster flights and prey transfers high in the air.

**Date and Location Seen:** _____

Immature

**Description:** 30 cm, wingspan 61 cm (averages; female larger than male). **Small**, slim, short-winged hawk with long, **matchstick-thin yellow legs**, broadly banded, **long, square-tipped tail**. Alternates rapid flapping with gliding. ADULT: Barred reddish-brown below, head, back dark grey, eye red. IMMATURE: Brownish back, streaked brown-and-white below. JUVENILE: Eye yellow.

**Similar Species:** Cooper's Hawk (page 123) nearly identical, but larger, tail rounder at tip; adult has "capped," sometimes square-headed appearance. Size separation tricky—female Sharp-shinned barely smaller than male Cooper's. American Kestrel (page 129), Merlin (page 131) have pointed wings.

**Seasonal Abundance:** Fairly common migrant in region, less common in winter; uncommon breeder. Ranges from Alaska to Labrador, winters south to Central America.

**Where to Find:** Throughout region.

**Habitat:** Breeds in dense coniferous or mixed forest. Migrants, winter birds in broken woodland, brushy areas, neighbourhoods.

**Diet and Behaviour:** Feeds almost exclusively on birds, often near bird feeders. Bursts forth from hidden perch to surprise prey in low, rapid flight. Often shadows migrating songbird flocks. Pugnacious if concealed nest discovered.

**Voice:** High-pitched *kew*, given in series.

**Did you know?** Many Sharp-shinned Hawks remain year round in their breeding range, but disperse widely in fall using thermals to assist travel and to locate prey while soaring.

**Date and Location Seen:** _____

Immature

**Description:** 43 cm, wingspan 84 cm (averages; female larger than male). Lanky, short-winged hawk, **long, yellow, pencil-sized legs, long, broadly banded tail**. Soars with wings held straight across. ADULT: Barred reddish-brown below, **dark grey cap**, greyish back, pale grey neck, eye reddish. IMMATURE: Brown back, white with brown streaks below. JUVENILE: Eye yellow.

**Similar Species:** Sharp-shinned Hawk (page 121) almost identical but smaller, with thinner legs, tail squarer at tip. Adult lacks "capped" appearance, soars with wrists held forward. Size separation tricky—male Cooper's only slightly larger than female Sharp-shinned. Red-tailed Hawk (page 125) lacks broad tail bands. Northern Goshawk (not shown; rare in region) adult grey, immature heavily streaked to undertail.

**Seasonal Abundance:** Fairly common migrant, resident in region. Secretive nester, much more evident in other seasons. Ranges across continent, southern Canada to Central America.

**Where to Find:** Throughout region.

**Habitat:** Forest, broken woodland, farms, neighbourhoods.

**Diet and Behaviour:** Ambushes prey from hidden perch with rapid burst of speed, also cruises, searches; often stakes out bird feeders. Takes mostly birds, also small mammals while nesting. Disperses widely in fall although many remain year round in breeding range.

**Voice:** Calls include repeated *kek*, nasal squawks.

**Did you know?** About 30 pairs of Cooper's Hawks nest in Greater Victoria, one of the species' highest known breeding densities.

**Date and Location Seen:** _____

**Immature**

**Description:** 51 cm, wingspan 122 cm. Bulky. Soars on **broad wings** held flat. **Dark line on leading edge of underwing** from neck to wrist, **dark head**, streaked band across belly. ADULT: Reddish tail. IMMATURE: Brown, finely banded tail, whiter breast. DARK MORPH: Adult brown except lighter flight feathers. HARLAN'S: Usually blackish, lacks brown tones; tail whitish.

**Similar Species:** Rough-legged Hawk (page 127) has white tail with broad black tip, whitish head, dark wrist marks on underwings, soars with wings held above horizontal. Eagles (page 117) have longer wings.

**Seasonal Abundance:** Most common, widespread hawk in region, numbers augmented by migrants, wintering birds. Dark morph uncommon, Harlan's rare winter visitor. Ranges across North America south of treeline, to Central America.

**Where to Find:** Nearly anywhere.

**Habitat:** Open habitats, edges—highly adaptable. Fields, highway corridors, clear-cuts, open woods.

**Diet and Behaviour:** Hunts for wide variety of prey, mostly from perch, swooping to capture prey in talons. Also soars, sometimes "kites" in stationary hover in wind. Will take carrion. Protects territory year round, calling at intruders.

**Voice:** Most common call rasping, down-slurred scream.

**Did you know?** Red-tailed Hawks come in an amazing assortment of plumages. Variation among regional populations, colour morphs, ages, and even individuals can make this common species difficult to identify.

**Date and Location Seen:** _____

Light Morph

Immature Light Morph

Dark Morph

**Description:** 53 cm, wingspan 135 cm. Broad-winged, bulky, soaring hawk with **highly variable** plumage dependent on sex, age, colour morph. Key marks include **white tail with wide black tip, whitish head** with dark eye-line, small bill, white upper breast, dark belly, white underwings with **dark wrist patches**. Less common dark morph appears blackish except for white flight feathers contrasting with front of underwing.

**Similar Species:** Red-tailed Hawk (page 125) immature may appear similar, especially when hovering, but wings less pointed, held flatter; underwing lacks wrist mark, instead has dark line on leading edge.

**Seasonal Abundance:** Fairly common but local winter resident in region, arrives October, departs by April. Breeds on Arctic tundra in North America, Eurasia, winters to temperate latitudes.

**Where to Find:** Winters in lowlands but migrants also use mountains. Reliable only in Fraser Valley, especially Fraser Delta.

**Habitat:** Agricultural fields, marshes.

**Diet and Behaviour:** Hunts mostly for small mammals from perch or by hovering in place; also takes birds, carrion. Soars with wings held above horizontal. Often perches on twigs that appear small for its bulk. Sometimes forms communal roosts in winter.

**Voice:** Seldom heard in winter.

**Did you know?** Rough-legged Hawk is the only hawk in southwestern British Columbia with feathered ("rough") legs.

**Date and Location Seen:** _____

Male

Female

**Description:** 25 cm, wingspan 53 cm. **Delicate**, long-tailed falcon with **russet back**, grey-and-rufous crown, **two black stripes on white face**. MALE: Long, **pointed wings**, blue-grey above, solid russet tail ending in wide black band, narrow white tip. Breast rusty in adult, streaked in immature. FEMALE: Similar; wings, tail russet with fine banding, breast streaked.

**Similar Species:** Merlin (page 131) chunkier; darkly streaked below with broadly banded tail, vague moustache mark, more powerful flight.

**Seasonal Abundance:** Generally uncommon at best in region except during migration, when sometimes fairly common locally. Ranges across North America south of treeline, winters as far south as Central America.

**Where to Find:** Sparsely distributed in lowlands, also mountains in summer.

**Habitat:** Open areas such as farmland, alpine meadows, forest edges, clearings.

**Diet and Behaviour:** Hunts for insects, small mammals, small birds, from perches or by stationary hovering over field. Nests in natural cavities (usually trees) but also uses nest boxes. Defends territory by calling, flying at intruders.

**Voice:** Common call series of piercing *kli* notes.

**Did you know?** American Kestrels are highly migratory. Winter residents in southwestern British Columbia may be migrants from farther north, while summer residents may go south.

**Date and Location Seen:** _____

**Description:** 28 cm, wingspan 58 cm. Compact, **swift-flying**, small falcon. Plumage varies with race, but generally **heavily streaked below** with plain, dark back, **banded tail, vague moustache mark**. Appears dark in flight with **sharply pointed wings**. MALE: Adult with grey back, cap. FEMALE: Larger, browner. JUVENILE: Brown.

**Similar Species:** Peregrine Falcon (page 133) larger with prominent moustache mark. American Kestrel (page 129) lighter below, finely built, with distinct head markings.

**Seasonal Abundance:** Fairly common but easily overlooked migrant, winter resident in region; rare breeder. Ranges across northern forests of Eurasia, North America, winters to southern tropics.

**Where to Find:** Mostly lowlands. Easiest to find in cities, towns, or near coastal concentrations of Dunlins.

**Habitat:** Coastal marshes, agricultural flats, broken woodlands, urban areas.

**Diet and Behaviour:** Makes dashing flights from perch, captures prey with talons at blinding speed. Diet almost exclusively small songbirds, shorebirds. Rarely soars; typical flight observation bullet-like pass. More likely spotted perched atop prominent snags, conifers. Aggressively harasses other raptors many times its size.

**Voice:** Rarely vocal away from nest; calls include series of *twi* notes.

**Did you know?** Merlins are rare breeders in coastal mountain forests. Nesting reports from the lowlands of the region, including cities, are increasing.

**Date and Location Seen:** _____

Immature

**Description:** 41 cm, wingspan 109 cm. Sleek, powerfully built, **crow-sized** falcon with **thick moustache mark**, long **wings reaching tail tip when perched**. Grey above, dark barring below, variable salmon-coloured or whitish bib. **Sharply pointed wings** in flight. IMMATURE: Browner with streaking instead of barring; bill, skin around eye pale blue (yellow in adult).

**Similar Species:** Merlin (page 131) smaller, moustache mark less distinct. Two other falcons rare in region (not shown). Prairie Falcon browner with dark armpits; Gyrfalcon bulkier with shorter, broader wings.

**Seasonal Abundance:** Uncommon resident in region, numbers augmented by migrants, wintering birds late September–May. Many races range worldwide.

**Where to Find:** Most common in lowlands; nests on coastal islands as well as on mainland cliffs. Best bets around wintering concentrations of waterfowl, shorebirds—e.g., Fraser Delta.

**Habitat:** Seacoasts, cities, agricultural fields, tidal flats. Requires cliffs, buildings, other tall structures for nesting, often near water.

**Diet and Behaviour:** Catches live birds in mid-air, making spectacular dives at speeds over 300 kilometres per hour. Prey ranges from songbirds to ducks; Rock Pigeons, shorebirds favoured. Rarely eats mammals, carrion. Nests on bare ledge, fiercely defends territory.

**Voice:** Calls include harsh, piercing series of *keh* notes.

**Did you know?** While Peregrine Falcon populations plummeted across North America in the 1950s due to DDT pollution, numbers on the British Columbia coast remained fairly stable.

**Date and Location Seen:** _____

Sora

**Description:** 25 cm. Long-legged marsh bird with **reddish-brown breast**, grey face, **long, thin, slightly downcurved red bill**, banded black-and-white flanks, short tail (often cocked upward). JUVENILE: Smaller, blacker, less colourful.

**Similar Species: Sora** (see inset; uncommon summer resident in region) similar in size, behaviour, habitat preferences, but has **grey breast, shorter, thicker yellow bill, black face**.

**Seasonal Abundance:** Fairly common summer resident in region; most leave September, return March. Locally fairly common winter resident in ice-free marshes. Breeds across much of North America from southern Canada south; winters along coasts, in Mexico. Also resident in South America.

**Where to Find:** Anywhere in lowlands with suitable habitat, e.g., Jericho Park, Buttertubs Marsh, Pitt Meadows, Rithets Bog.

**Habitat:** Pond edges, estuaries, marshes (freshwater or brackish), even roadside ditches. Needs shallow standing water, emergent vegetation, lots of edges.

**Diet and Behaviour:** Largely animal diet—insects, larvae, snails, spiders, small frogs, small fish; some vegetal material. Probes with bill in mud, shallow water, dead vegetation. Rarely seen flying; mostly runs or walks, staying well hidden.

**Voice:** Calls include *kiddik kiddik kiddik* in breeding season; series of quacking grunts, often in duet, throughout year.

**Did you know?** Virginia Rails have flexible vertebrae to help them thread their way through dense standing vegetation, and long toes for walking on floating mats.

**Date and Location Seen:** _____

**Description:** 38 cm, wingspan 66 cm. **Dark grey** aquatic bird, undertail edged in white. Black head, red iris, **pointed white bill with band near tip**, white forehead shield (dark red or brown at top). Legs greenish to yellowish, **long-lobed toes**. JUVENILE: Paler, legs grey, no red on forehead shield.

**Similar Species:** Distinctive. Pied-billed Grebe (page 95) brown.

**Seasonal Abundance:** Fairly common summer resident in region, common winter resident (September–March). Nests western half of North America, Midwest; winters along coasts, in southern U.S., south to Costa Rica.

**Where to Find:** Widespread in lowlands; summers wherever it finds suitable marsh habitat. Large numbers in winter at Esquimalt Lagoon, Elk Lake, Reifel Sanctuary, Iona Island, Cranberry Lake in Powell River.

**Habitat:** Breeds in shallow freshwater lakes, wetlands with emergent vegetation, open water. Winters on lakes, ponds, protected saltwater bays.

**Diet and Behaviour:** Dives or tips up in shallow water, grazes on lawns, fields. Eats mostly plants, a few invertebrates. Needs long takeoff path, splashing strides on water, until airborne.

**Voice:** *Puck* notes singly or in series; array of other cackling, clucking, crowing calls.

**Did you know?** Wigeons and Gadwalls often swim with American Coots, wait for them to surface, and steal the aquatic vegetation they bring up.

**Date and Location Seen:** _____

Breeding

Non-breeding

**Description:** 28 cm. Plump, with **short bill**, relatively short, blackish legs; **black armpits** visible in flight. BREEDING: Adults show **black face, breast, belly**, whitish crown, neck, sides, undertail, spangled back. Female, moulting birds browner, less distinctly marked. NON-BREEDING: Speckled brownish-grey above with indistinct whitish eyebrow, plainer below. JUVENILE: Browner with greyish legs.

**Similar Species:** Distinctive in breeding plumage, bill shorter than other large shorebirds. American, Pacific Golden-Plovers (neither shown; both rare in region) slightly smaller, lack black armpit; more golden in summer, browner in fall.

**Seasonal Abundance:** Fairly common migrant, winter resident in region. Breeds on Arctic tundra around northern hemisphere, winters to southern continents.

**Where to Find:** Lowlands, mostly coastal; locally common on Fraser Delta, Boundary Bay.

**Habitat:** Mud flats, shortgrass or plowed fields, beaches, open marsh.

**Diet and Behaviour:** Forages visually by running, stopping, picking food from ground; also may probe. Diet mostly worms, insects, marine organisms. Birds spread out to feed but roost in groups, often flocking with other shorebirds, especially Dunlins.

**Voice:** Very vocal. Most common call forlorn-sounding, whistled *plee o weee.*

**Did you know?** This widespread species is known in Eurasia as the Grey Plover.

**Date and Location Seen:** _____

**Description:** 18 cm. Plain greyish-brown above except for **white-and-black collar, forehead**, black cheek; **white below with black breast band. Bill short** with pinkish-orange base; pinkish-yellow legs short. White wing stripe on long wings visible in flight. JUVENILE: Duller with dark bill.

**Similar Species:** Shorter bill separates from sandpipers. Killdeer (page 143) larger with double breast band; juvenile Killdeer usually appears fluffy.

**Seasonal Abundance:** Fairly common but local migrant in region, arrives mid-July, most gone by October. Returns late April–May. Breeds across North American Arctic, Subarctic, winters as far south as South America.

**Where to Find:** Lowlands; widespread along marine shores, especially common on Fraser Delta.

**Habitat:** Wide-open places; prefers marine environments such as tidal flats, mud flats, beaches. Also agricultural fields (flooded, plowed), pond margins.

**Diet and Behaviour:** Forages visually by running, stopping, picking food from ground. Feeds on marine organisms, insects. Usually in flocks, associates loosely with other shorebirds.

**Voice:** Common flight call whistled *chu wee*. Trills, chatters during interactions with others of its species.

**Did you know?** Semipalmated Plover gets its name from its partially webbed feet.

**Date and Location Seen:** _____

**Description:** 25 cm. Plain brown above with white collar, **white below except for two black breast bands**. Forehead, eyebrow white; **bill dark, short**; legs relatively short, yellowish. **Orange tail, rump**, white wing stripe visible in flight. Scarlet eye-ring. JUVENILE: One breast band when half-grown.

**Similar Species:** Semi-palmated Plover (page 141) smaller with one breast band, shorter bill, lacks orange rump.

**Seasonal Abundance:** Common summer resident in region, less common in winter. Ranges from Alaska, Newfoundland to South America; withdraws from coldest areas in winter.

**Where to Find:** Mostly lowlands, also up major river valleys to moderate elevations.

**Habitat:** Open habitats without high grass: lawns, road edges, beaches, mud flats, plowed fields, parking lots. Prefers bare gravel for nesting.

**Diet and Behaviour:** Forages visually by running, stopping, picking food from ground. Feeds mostly on insects, also some seeds. Secretive at open nest site but calls, feigns broken wing as part of distraction display when discovered. Flocks concentrate in farm fields in late summer.

**Voice:** Varied strident calls include *kill deeah, deee, dee ahy*. Gives high, rapid trill when nervous.

**Did you know?** The Killdeer's four black-spotted eggs are nearly invisible in their gravel nest when left unattended.

**Date and Location Seen:** _____

**Description:** 43 cm. **Chunky, all-black** shorebird with long, chisel-like, **bright red bill**, eye-ring. Pinkish-yellow, relatively short legs, golden eye. JUVENILE: Duller, with dark-tipped, dull red bill.

**Similar Species:** None in region.

**Seasonal Abundance:** Uncommon resident in region. Ranges along Pacific Coast from southern Alaska to Baja California.

**Where to Find:** Limited to rocky coastline. Good spots include Clover Point in Victoria, Esquimalt Lagoon, Lighthouse Park in West Vancouver, Tsawwassen ferry jetty.

**Habitat:** Rocky shores, islets, cobble beaches, jetties, breakwaters.

**Diet and Behaviour:** Forages mostly when tide low, primarily for mussels, other shellfish. Uses laterally compressed bill to pry shells apart. Also feeds on other marine organisms. Usually in pairs or family groups, but also forms small flocks outside breeding season. Non-migratory, but disperses infrequently to coastal localities away from nesting grounds. May roost with bill tucked under wing—less easily identified then.

**Voice:** Loud, ringing yelps, whistles; rolling series given in display.

**Did you know?** Black Oystercatcher populations increased significantly in the 1990s in the southern Strait of Georgia, including the Vancouver area, and are considered stable along the rest of the British Columbia coast.


**Date and Location Seen:** _____

**Greater Yellowlegs
Breeding**

**Greater Yellowlegs
Juvenile**

**Lesser Yellowlegs
Breeding**

**Lesser Yellowlegs
Juvenile**

**Description:** 36 cm / 25 cm. Elegant, greyish waders with long, **bright yellowish-orange legs**, long neck, fairly long, mostly dark bill, whitish speckling on dark back. Lighter below, with **plain wings, white rump** visible in flight. Breast streaked in breeding plumage. GREATER: More robust, thicker legs, **bill longer, slightly upturned**, pale-based. LESSER: More **delicate; bill shorter, straighter**; less likely in saltwater habitat.

**Similar Species:** Solitary Sandpiper (not shown; rare in region) slightly smaller than Lesser, with greenish legs, white eye-ring.

**Seasonal Abundance:** Fairly common migrants in region. GREATER: Arrives July, a few linger in winter; returns March–May. Breeds southern Alaska, central British Columbia to Labrador, winters to South America. LESSER: Arrives by July, departs by October, rarely winters; uncommon in spring. Breeds Alaska, northern Canada, winters to South America.

**Where to Find:** Lowlands.

**Habitat:** Flooded fields, marshes, ponds, estuaries, tidal flats.

**Diet and Behaviour:** Forage in shallow water, swinging bill side to side or running after small fish, insects, other organisms; often flock, sometimes with other shorebirds.

**Voice:** Call *tew*, repeated three to four times in GREATER, two to three times in LESSER; both *tew* continuously in alarm.

**Did you know?** In British Columbia, Greater Yellowlegs nests in the Cariboo–Chilcotin region, Lesser in the northern third of the province.

**Date and Location Seen:** _____

Breeding

Non-breeding

**Description:** 29 cm. Stocky **all-grey** shorebird with relatively **short yellow legs**, longish bill. **Bobs constantly**. BREEDING: Heavily barred below. NON-BREEDING: Clear grey breast, white belly.

**Similar Species:** Yellowlegs (page 147) with longer legs, finer bill, generally found on muddy or sandy shores. Surfbird (page 157) has short bill with pale base, striking black-and-white flight pattern. Spotted Sandpiper (page 151) shows same bobbing habit, but smaller, browner, with white breast.

**Seasonal Abundance:** Fairly common migrant in region, late April–May, July–September. Breeds northern British Columbia, Yukon, Alaska; winters on Pacific Coast of South America.

**Where to Find:** Strictly salt water; more common on outer coasts where large waves break over rocks; rare on mainland. Good sites include Pacific Rim National Park; Ogden, Clover, McMicking points in Victoria.

**Habitat:** Wave-washed, rocky marine shorelines, including rock jetties.

**Diet and Behaviour:** Forages, usually singly, among rocks in intertidal zone for small molluscs, crabs, amphipods, other invertebrates.

**Voice:** High-pitched piping call.

**Did you know?** Wandering Tattlers nest along gravelly rivers in northern mountains, including a small breeding population in extreme northwestern British Columbia.

**Date and Location Seen:** _____

Breeding

Non-breeding

**Description:** 20 cm. Small, with **short reddish bill**, short yellowish legs, **white wing stripe** visible in flight, white eye-line, **constant teetering motion**. BREEDING: **Dark spots** on white underparts, bill brighter red. NON-BREEDING: Evenly greyish-brown above to dusky neck; **white underparts extend up side in front of folded wing**. JUVENILE: White edges on wing feathers.

**Similar Species:** Solitary Sandpiper (not shown; rare in region) also teeters; taller, with greenish legs, fine white back spotting, strong white eye-ring, lacks black eye-line.

**Seasonal Abundance:** Fairly common summer resident in region; rare in winter. Ranges across North America, winters to South America.

**Where to Find:** Widespread, from lowlands to mountains.

**Habitat:** Nests along ponds, rivers, mountain streams, other fresh water in open or wooded terrain. In migration, frequents pebbly pond edges, coastline, mud flats, sewage ponds.

**Diet and Behaviour:** Forages visually by picking, chasing, fluttering after insects, small organisms, tiny fish; may take carrion. Highly territorial at all seasons so does not flock. Distinctive flight: short pulses with wings not raised above horizontal, alternating with glides on bowed wings.

**Voice:** Loud, repeated, clear, high-pitched whistles.

**Did you know?** Spotted Sandpiper females sometimes mate with more than one male, a rare mating system called polyandry found in a small number of other shorebird species.

**Date and Location Seen:** _____

Marbled Godwit

**Description:** 43 cm. **Large**, with long, greyish legs, **long, downcurved bill, bold brown-and-buff head stripes**. Overall greyish-brown with whitish belly; back mottled, streaked. All plumages similar.

**Similar Species:** Long-billed Curlew (not shown; rare in region) larger, longer-billed, with cinnamon underwings (barred brownish in Whimbrel). **Marbled Godwit** (see inset; rare in region) similar in size with **long, upturned bill**.

**Seasonal Abundance:** Fairly common migrant in region, especially on west coast of Vancouver Island; very rare winter resident. Late-spring migrants pass through in early June, earliest fall birds return later that month. Breeds around northern hemisphere on Arctic tundra, winters coastally to tropics.

**Where to Find:** Seashores, especially mud flats, beaches on west coast of Vancouver Island (e.g., Grice Bay); also Fraser Delta. Often roosts on offshore islands.

**Habitat:** Plowed agricultural fields, mud flats, rocky shores, marshes, meadows.

**Diet and Behaviour:** Forages by walking, picks or probes just below surface for worms, crabs, other invertebrates; may eat some plant material. Large spring flocks drawn to newly plowed fields; fall migrants alone or in smaller groups may flock with other shorebirds, usually at coast.

**Voice:** Common call loud *whi whi whi whi whi* whistle, also other trills, whistles in spring.

**Did you know?** The Eurasian race of the Whimbrel has a white rump.

**Date and Location Seen:** _____

**Breeding**

**Ruddy Turnstone Breeding**

**Ruddy Turnstone Non-breeding**

**Non-breeding**

**Description:** 23 cm. Stocky with brownish legs, short, black **chisel-like bill**, black **tail with white base. White back, wing stripe, underwing, shoulder patch visible in flight**. BREEDING: Black above; white patches above, below eye; white belly. NON-BREEDING: Browner above, without face markings. JUVENILE: As non-breeding.

**Similar Species:** Larger Surfbird (page 157) lacks white back patches in flight. **Ruddy Turnstone** (see insets; less common in region) has **reddish legs, harlequin pattern** (rufous-black-white) in breeding plumage; dull brown in winter.

**Seasonal Abundance:** Fairly common migrant, winter resident in region from mid-July through April. Breeds coastal Alaskan tundra, winters on coast from southeastern Alaska to Mexico.

**Where to Find?** Coastline, e.g., Clover Point, Victoria; Piper's Lagoon, Nanaimo; Cypress Creek mouth, West Vancouver.

**Habitat:** Rocky shores, breakwaters, log booms, occasionally beaches, mud flats.

**Diet and Behaviour:** Forages on rocks, prying off mussels, other marine organisms; also turns rocks, shells to search beneath; may feed on carrion, plant material. Roosts, feeds in flocks, often with other shorebirds, particularly Surfbirds.

**Voice:** Highly vocal, with shrill rattles, chatter—especially when flushed.

**Did you know?** More wary than Surfbirds, Black Turnstones act as sentinels for both species, calling frequently in alarm.

**Date and Location Seen:** _____

Non-breeding

Non-breeding

**Description:** 25 cm. Dark, **stocky**, with short yellowish legs, **short bill** (blackish with yellow base), broad white wing stripe, **white tail with broad black band at tip**. BREEDING: Rufous highlights on back feathers; heavily marked with dark chevrons on white belly, flanks. NON-BREEDING: Evenly greyish-brown with fewer marks on belly. JUVENILE: May appear browner.

**Similar Species:** Black Turnstone (page 155) smaller with white on back, inner wing. Wandering Tattler (page 149) has longer, all-dark bill, lacks black-and-white pattern in flight. Rock Sandpiper (not shown; uncommon in region in winter on rocky marine shores) smaller with dark rump, longer, pointed bill.

**Seasonal Abundance:** Fairly common migrant, winter resident in region (mid-July–April). Breeds on alpine tundra of Alaska, Yukon, winters on Pacific Coast from Alaska south to Chile.

**Where to Find:** Rocky coastlines of Vancouver Island, Sunshine Coast, Lower Howe Sound.

**Habitat:** Rocky shores, jetties; rarely on sand, mud flats.

**Diet and Behaviour:** Forages by pulling mussels, barnacles, other marine organisms from rocks. Roosts, feeds in flocks, almost always with other rock-loving shorebirds, particularly Black Turnstones. Often allows close approach.

**Voice:** Seldom vocal in region; occasional high squeaks, chatter.

**Did you know?** The nesting grounds of the Surfbird on remote ridgetops and mountains remained undiscovered until the 1920s.

**Date and Location Seen:** _____

Breeding

Non-breeding

**Description:** 19 cm. Small but **stout**, with black, relatively short, **straight, blunt-tipped bill**, short black legs. In flight, broad **white wing stripe** contrasts with dark flight feathers. BREEDING: Upperparts **rufous**, underparts white. NON-BREEDING: **Pale grey above** with clean white underparts. JUVENILE: Upperparts more spangled with blackish, may show some buff below.

**Similar Species:** Other small shorebirds darker than Sanderling in non-breeding plumage. Bright breeding plumage unique (seen only late spring in region).

**Seasonal Abundance:** Fairly common migrant, winter resident in region (August–May). Breeds on high Arctic tundra around northern hemisphere, winters from Alaska to southernmost parts of southern continents.

**Where to Find:** Coastal; rare away from salt water. Boundary Bay, Ogden Point, Esquimalt Lagoon, Grice Bay good bets.

**Habitat:** Beaches, sometimes mud flats.

**Diet and Behaviour:** Actively forages on beach just above waves, running with legs moving rapidly like windup toy. Picks, probes for small marine organisms on sand or mud, may eat some carrion. Roosts, feeds in flocks, sometimes with other shorebirds.

**Voice:** Most common call sharp *kip*.

**Did you know?** Sanderlings that winter in the southern hemisphere may fly over 13,000 kilometres to reach their nesting grounds in spring.

**Date and Location Seen:** _____

**Semipalmated Sandpiper**

Breeding

Non-breeding

Juvenile

**Description:** 16 cm. Small sandpiper, brownish-grey with evenly tapered, **drooping, fine-tipped bill, blackish legs**, white belly, whitish eye-line; thin white wing stripe visible in flight. BREEDING: **Rufous highlights in back, head feathers**, black chevron marks on flanks. NON-BREEDING: Evenly greyish-brown with white underparts. JUVENILE: Paler, less strongly marked than breeding adult.

**Similar Species: Semipalmated Sandpiper** (see inset; rare in region) has **blunt, short bill, little or no rufous colouring**. Baird's Sandpiper (not shown; uncommon fall migrant in region) slightly larger with thin, straight bill, folded wings longer than tail. Sanderling (page 159) larger, with shorter, blunt bill. Least Sandpiper (page 163) has yellowish legs.

**Seasonal Abundance:** Common migrant in region July–November; a few winter. Breeding-plumaged flocks present spring, early summer. Breeds Alaska west to Siberia, winters coastally to South America.

**Where to Find:** Throughout lowlands, mostly coastal.

**Habitat:** Open shoreline, mud flats, muddy fields, tidal estuaries.

**Diet and Behaviour:** Probes, picks small organisms from mud while wading, walking; may eat seeds. Feeds, roosts in flocks with other shorebirds.

**Voice:** Flight call thin *dcheet*. Feeding flocks may chatter.

**Did you know?** Western Sandpiper is the most abundant migrant shorebird on the British Columbia coast. Spring counts on the Fraser Delta have reached 1 million per day.

**Date and Location Seen:** _____

Breeding

Non-breeding

Juvenile

**Description:** 14 cm. **Smallest sandpiper**, brownish with **short, fine-tipped, drooping bill, yellowish legs, brownish upper breast**, white belly, white lines down back; thin white wing stripe visible in flight. BREEDING: Darker with black centers on back feathers. NON-BREEDING: Evenly greyish brown with whitish belly. JUVENILE: More rufous than adult, legs duller.

**Similar Species:** Western, Semipalmated Sandpipers (both page 161), Baird's Sandpiper (not shown; uncommon fall migrant in region) have blackish legs. Baird's larger with thin, straight bill. Pectoral Sandpiper (page 165) similar but much larger, legs proportionally longer.

**Seasonal Abundance:** Common migrant in region July–October, less common April–May. A few winter. Breeds Alaska–Labrador, winters to northern South America.

**Where to Find:** Throughout region, mostly in lowlands.

**Habitat:** Mud flats, pond margins, marshes, coastal bays, muddy pools, ditches.

**Diet and Behaviour:** Forages mostly by picking, sometimes probing, primarily for insects, aquatic organisms; may eat some plant material. Frequently in small groups rather than large flocks. Not shy, often allowing close approach.

**Voice:** Flight call *pree eet*. Birds may utter *dee dee dee* call among themselves.

**Did you know?** The small North American sandpipers (including Least and Western) are often referred to collectively as "peeps," together with the stints of Eurasia.

**Date and Location Seen:** _____

**Description:** 23 cm. **Medium-sized**, streaky, brownish sandpiper, with moderately heavy, slightly drooping bill, **yellowish legs**. Greyish-brown **upper breast abruptly contrasts with white belly**. Long, dark wings show only weak, light stripe in flight.

**Similar Species:** Least Sandpiper (page 163) similar, but much smaller with less distinct lower breast border. Baird's Sandpiper (not shown; uncommon fall migrant in region) smaller with dark legs, straight bill. Sharp-tailed Sandpiper (not shown; rare fall migrant in region) with distinct reddish cap, peachy-buff breast. Dowitchers (page 169) have much longer bills.

**Seasonal Abundance:** Rare to uncommon spring migrant (May), common fall migrant (July–early November). Breeds on tundra from eastern Siberia to central Canada, winters to South America.

**Where to Find:** Widespread; mainly lowlands.

**Habitat:** Open flats, plowed farm fields, marshes, wet meadows, grassy spots along pond margins.

**Diet and Behaviour:** Picks, probes, primarily for insects, aquatic organisms. Tends to forage quietly in small groups in or close to vegetation on drier parts of flats; detection difficult at times.

**Voice:** Low, harsh, reedy *drrrit* in flight.

**Did you know?** Male Pectoral Sandpipers have air sacs in their chest that they inflate during courtship displays.

**Date and Location Seen:** _____

Breeding

Non-breeding

**Description:** 21.5 cm. Fairly small, **hunched appearance**, with **short, dark legs, long, dark bill with drooping tip**; white wing stripe visible in flight. BREEDING: Spring birds mostly **rufous above with black belly**, whitish face, upper breast. NON-BREEDING: **Plain brownish-grey** with white belly, underwing, faint eye-line.

**Similar Species:** Larger with longer bill than other small shorebirds. Smaller size, drooping bill separate Dunlin from dowitchers (page 169).

**Seasonal Abundance:** Common migrant, winter resident in region, arrives late in fall (mostly October). Attains breeding plumage by April, departs by early May. Breeds on tundra around northern hemisphere, winters south from temperate latitudes to subtropics.

**Where to Find:** Throughout lowlands; abundant on Fraser Delta, Boundary Bay, where flocks number in tens of thousands.

**Habitat:** Coastal bays, tidal flats, muddy fields, rarely far from salt water.

**Diet and Behaviour:** Forages by picking, probing mud, primarily for aquatic organisms; may eat some plant material. Tight, swirling flocks move with mechanized precision, alternately flashing white, grey; large numbers in distance may appear to be smoke.

**Voice:** Flight call harsh *kreev*.

**Did you know?** Formerly known as Red-backed Sandpiper in reference to its bright spring colour, the Dunlin derives its current name from the "dun" plumage it wears for most of the year.

## Date and Location Seen: _____

**Short-billed Dowitcher Breeding**

**Short-billed Dowitcher Juvenile**

**Long-billed Dowitcher Breeding**

**Long-billed Dowitcher Non-breeding**

**Description:** 28 cm. Stocky. **Long, straight bill, white wedge on back**, finely banded tail, greenish legs, mostly dark wings, **whitish eye-line. Rusty breast in breeding plumage**, overall greyish in winter. SHORT-BILLED: Summer–fall juvenile has **bright golden markings near tip of folded wing**. LONG-BILLED: Underparts entirely rusty in breeding plumage (Short-billed has white belly).

**Similar Species:** Longer bill than similarly sized shorebirds except Wilson's Snipe (page 171) which has white stripes on head, back. Stilt Sandpiper (not shown; rare fall migrant in region) smaller, proportionally longer-legged, may feed with dowitchers.

**Seasonal Abundance:** Fairly common migrants in region. SHORT-BILLED: Arrives late June, departs by October, back April–May. Breeds Canada, Alaska, winters to South America. LONG-BILLED: Arrives July, a few winter; numbers increase into May. Breeds northwestern North America, northeastern Siberia, winters to Mexico.

**Where to Find:** Lowlands; Reifel Sanctuary, Iona Island good bets.

**Habitat:** Mud flats, marshes, pools. SHORT-BILLED prefers tidal flats, LONG-BILLED fresh water.

**Diet and Behaviour:** Probe mud like sewing machine, primarily for aquatic organisms, also plant material. Usually flock, often with other shorebirds.

**Voice:** SHORT-BILLED: Low, liquid, whistled *tlu tu tu*, given in flight. LONG-BILLED: Sharp *keek*, sometimes in rapid series.

**Did you know?** The two species are difficult to separate. Bill length averages longer for Long-billed but there is much overlap.

**Date and Location Seen:** _____

169

**Description:** 25 cm. Stocky. Mostly brown with **long, straight bill**, short, greenish legs, dark wings, **rust-orange tail, white lower breast, belly**. Bold **whitish streaks on head, face, back**, dark bars along flanks. Formerly known as Common Snipe.

**Similar Species:** Much longer bill than other similarly sized shorebirds except dowitchers (page 169), which lack white stripes on head, back.

**Seasonal Abundance:** Fairly common migrant, winter resident in region (July–May); rare breeder. Ranges across North America, winters to northern South America.

**Where to Find:** Throughout lowlands, up to moderate elevations.

**Habitat:** Wet ground including marshes, bogs, flooded fields, margins of ponds, streams.

**Diet and Behaviour:** Forages mostly for insects, worms, other organisms by probing mud, shallow water. Sits tight, relying on camouflage until approached closely, then flushes explosively. Often concentrates in loose flocks during migration. Male flies high in breeding display, with shallow dives during which vibrating tail feathers produce hollow whinny sound ("winnowing").

**Voice:** Abrupt rasping *skresh* uttered when flushed. Breeding call *chip a*, repeated many times from exposed perch.

**Did you know?** The eyes of the Wilson's Snipe are set well back on the sides of the head, enabling it literally to watch its back for danger even as it probes for food.

**Date and Location Seen:** _____

**Female Breeding**

**Juvenile**

**Description:** 18.5 cm. Small, **swimming shorebird** with straight, thin, black bill; white wing stripe visible in flight. BREEDING: Female with grey cap, white chin, reddish neck, gold-striped back, grey sides, white belly. Male similar but duller. NON-BREEDING: Grey- and white-striped above, plain white below, with dark cap, **thick, dark line behind eye**. Early-fall juveniles have gold-striped back.

**Similar Species:** Non-breeding Red Phalarope (page 397) plain grey back, thicker bill. Wilson's Phalarope (not shown; rare in region): dark stripe from bill down side of neck, no wing stripe.

**Seasonal Abundance:** Fairly common fall migrant in region, late July–October; less common spring migrant, mostly May. Breeds on tundra at high latitudes around northern hemisphere, winters in tropical oceans. Migrates primarily at sea.

**Where to Find:** Offshore or at sewage ponds. Clover Point in Victoria, Iona Island good bets.

**Habitat:** Salt water, especially along tide lines; less often fresh water including sewage ponds, flooded fields.

**Diet and Behaviour:** Feeds on open water while swimming, often in circles, picking insects, other small organisms from surface. Seldom occurs on land except while nesting.

**Voice:** Frequent *kit kit* call.

**Did you know?** The usual sexual roles are reversed in phalaropes, with the smaller, duller-plumaged male incubating the eggs and raising the young.

**Date and Location Seen:** _____

173

**Description:** 42 cm (adult 51 cm with tail). Gull-like seabird with dark back; **strong, fast flight**, showing **white flashes in wings**. ADULT: Central **tail feathers long, pointed**. Dark morph blackish brown all over except for white in wings. IMMATURE: Dark brown, striped neck, barred back, belly; lacks long tail feathers.

**Similar Species:** Heermann's Gull (page 179) lacks long tail feathers, white wing flash. Pomarine Jaeger (page 399) larger, central tail feathers blunt, twisted; rarely seen from land. Long-tailed Jaeger (not shown; migrates far offshore in region) smaller, tail feathers proportionally much longer.

**Seasonal Abundance:** Fairly common fall migrant (August–October), uncommon spring migrant (May) along coasts in region; a few non-breeders summer offshore. Breeds around world on Arctic tundra, winters on tropical, subtropical seas.

**Where to Find:** Marine shores throughout region; watch for it harassing flying flocks of terns, small gulls.

**Habitat:** Coastal bays, offshore waters.

**Diet and Behaviour:** Pursues Bonaparte's Gulls, Common Terns with powerful, falcon-like flight, steals food from them in mid-air. Feeds on lemmings, small birds on tundra breeding grounds.

**Voice:** Generally silent away from breeding grounds.

**Did you know?** Only about 14 percent of Parasitic Jaegers in British Columbia are dark-morph birds.

**Date and Location Seen:** _____

Breeding

Non-breeding

Immature

**Description:** 33 cm, wingspan 81 cm. **Petite** gull; transitions to full adult plumage over two years. White below, pearl-grey back, black bill, short red legs. Square tail, **upper surface of forewing white**, outer trailing edge black. BREEDING: **Head black**. NON-BREEDING: **Head white with black spot behind eye**. FIRST-YEAR: Black tail tip, wing pattern.

**Similar Species:** Common Tern (page 195), Arctic Tern (page 401) have strongly forked tail, black limited to cap. Franklin's Gull (not shown; rare in region) larger with darker back; juveniles, non-breeding-plumaged birds show dark half-hood.

**Seasonal Abundance:** Common migrant in region. Spring birds peak March–April, continue through June; fall movement begins by July, peaks October–November. Good numbers winter, so present year round. Breeds northern North America, winters to Mexico.

**Where to Find:** Throughout lowlands, mostly near coast; migrants also along rivers, rarely at higher elevations. Spectacular April–May concentrations at Active Pass.

**Habitat:** Mostly coastal habitats, sewage lagoons; also rivers, lakes.

**Diet and Behaviour:** Forages for small fish, crustaceans, insects by plunge-diving or picking at water surface. Concentrates, occasionally in flocks of thousands, at sewage ponds, tidal rips.

**Voice:** Call unlike that of most gulls—low, harsh, grating *geerr*.

**Did you know?** Bonaparte's Gulls build their nests in coniferous trees around lakes in boreal forests.

**Date and Location Seen:** _____

Breeding

First-year

**Description:** 48 cm, wingspan 124 cm. Medium-sized gull; transitions to full adult plumage over three years. BREEDING: **Dark, unstreaked**; white head, **red bill**, light grey rump, underparts, **black tail with white tip**. NON-BREEDING: Head grey. FIRST-YEAR: Uniform dark brown with yellowish, black-tipped bill.

**Similar Species:** Distinctive in region. Other adult gulls white below, immatures streaked or mottled. Parasitic Jaeger (page 175), Pomarine Jaeger (page 399) falcon-like, plumage variable but always with white wing flash near tip.

**Seasonal Abundance:** Fairly common summer visitor in region (peak July–August), rare in other seasons. Breeds mainly Gulf of California, disperses along coast south to Guatemala, north to British Columbia.

**Where to Find:** Strictly coastal. Most common around southern Vancouver Island, Gulf Islands.

**Habitat:** Marine shores; shuns fresh water.

**Diet and Behaviour:** Forages mostly in flight over water for fish, small marine organisms; picks from surface or makes shallow dives. Gregarious. Moves en masse along coast after nesting.

**Voice:** Calls more nasal, hollow than those of other gulls.

**Did you know?** Heermann's Gull has a very restricted breeding range. Practically all of the world's population nests on one island—Isla Raza off the east coast of Baja California.

**Date and Location Seen:** _____

Breeding

Non-breeding

First-year

**Description:** 38 cm, wingspan 109 cm. Small gull; transitions to full adult plumage over three years. BREEDING: Tail, underparts white; back light slate-grey. White, **dove-like head, short yellowish bill, dark eye**, yellow legs. **Wingtips black with large white spots** near tip. NON-BREEDING: Head heavily streaked. FIRST-YEAR: Streaky brown with grey back, pink legs, dark eye, dark-tipped bill.

**Similar Species:** Smaller than most gulls in region. Adult darker grey, more white in wingtips than Ring-billed (page 183).

**Seasonal Abundance:** Common resident in region; more abundant, widespread in winter. Breeds on Harrison Lake, several Vancouver Island lakes, north to Alaska, northwestern Canada; winters southern Alaska to Baja California along Pacific Coast. Several other races in Eurasia.

**Where to Find:** Lowlands, mostly near coast.

**Habitat:** Coastal habitats, rivers (especially near mouths), lakes, sewage lagoons, agricultural fields.

**Diet and Behaviour:** Omnivorous; forages for worms in plowed fields; fish, marine organisms in coastal areas; insect larvae, waste in sewage ponds. May fly-catch during insect hatches. Gregarious; often flocks with other gulls, especially Ring-billeds.

**Voice:** Calls higher than those of other gulls, with mewed quality.

**Did you know?** The southernmost known Mew Gull breeding sites are in southwestern British Columbia.

**Date and Location Seen:** _____

**Breeding**

**First-year**

**Description:** 43 cm, wingspan 117 cm. **Medium-sized** gull; transitions to full adult plumage over three years. BREEDING: Pearl-grey back, white head, underparts, tail; **wingtips extensively black** with white spot near tip. **Yellow bill with black ring near tip**, yellow eye, legs. NON-BREEDING: Head streaked. FIRST-YEAR: Grey back, whitish underparts lightly scalloped with brown, dark eye, pink legs, dark-tipped bill.

**Similar Species:** Larger gulls have heavier bills. Adult Mew Gull (page 181) has smaller bill, darker back, whiter wingtips.

**Seasonal Abundance:** Common resident in region, although rarely nests. Ranges from southeastern Alaska to Labrador, south to Mexico, Caribbean.

**Where to Find:** Mostly mainland, rare at higher elevations.

**Habitat:** Coastal habitats, freshwater bodies, agricultural fields, urban settings including parking lots.

**Diet and Behaviour:** Omnivorous. Forages widely for fish; worms in plowed fields; refuse, scraps in cities. Often fly-catches during insect hatches, steals food from other birds. Long-lived, colonial nester with elaborate courtship, complex social behaviours. Gregarious, often flocks with other gulls.

**Voice:** Typical gull calls including long sequence of laugh-like squeals, beginning with long calls then trailing to shorter ones.

**Did you know?** Other gull species may have rings on their bills during winter and in transitional plumages. Take care not to confuse them with Ring-billed Gulls.

**Date and Location Seen:** _____

**Breeding**

**First-year**

**Description:** 51 cm, wingspan 135 cm. Fairly large gull; transitions to full adult plumage over four years. BREEDING: White head, underparts, tail; **light slate-grey back; wingtips black** with white near tip. Dark eye, **greenish-yellow legs,** fairly thin bill with **black-and-red spot near tip.** NON-BREEDING: Head streaked, legs greener. FIRST-YEAR: Streaky dark brown with some grey feathering (variable); pink legs, two-toned bill.

**Similar Species:** Only adult gull in region with yellowish legs, black-and-red spot on bill.

**Seasonal Abundance:** Uncommon winter–spring in region, becomes fairly common by summer, locally common late summer–fall as migrants arrive from breeding colonies on prairies. Breeds interior western North America, winters coastally British Columbia to Mexico.

**Where to Find:** Lowlands, but may be seen flying west over mountain passes in summer; common fall migrant offshore.

**Habitat:** Mostly coastal; also lakes, rivers, farms, cities.

**Diet and Behaviour:** Forages in coastal areas for fish, carrion, sometimes far from shore; in plowed fields for rodents, worms; in city refuse. May fly-catch, steal food from other birds. Often flocks with other gulls.

**Voice:** Typical for gull; can be harsh.

**Did you know?** California Gulls rescued Mormon settlers at the Great Salt Lake from the grasshopper plague of 1848.

**Date and Location Seen:** _____

**Non-breeding**

**First-year**

**Description:** 61 cm, wingspan 145 cm. Medium-large gull; transitions to full adult plumage over four years. BREEDING: Underparts, tail white, back **light grey, wingtips black with white tips**. Sloping forehead, relatively small, straight **bill with red spot** near tip, **pale yellow eye**, pink legs. NON-BREEDING: Head heavily streaked. FIRST-YEAR: Variably mottled dark brown with lighter head; eye dark, bill dark or two-toned.

**Similar Species:** Adult Thayer's Gull (page 189) has rounder head, wingtips blackish above but greyish below; most have dark eye. California Gull (page 185) adult with greenish-yellow legs. Hybrid Glaucous-winged × Western Gull (page 191) bill heavier, more angular.

**Seasonal Abundance:** Common migrant, winter resident on outer coast; uncommon around Strait of Georgia. Breeds around northern hemisphere, winters to tropics.

**Where to Find:** Most common on outer coast, including Pacific Rim National Park.

**Habitat:** Near water; beaches, mud flats; also landfills, urban areas, agricultural fields, golf courses, parking lots.

**Diet and Behaviour:** Omnivorous, forages mostly for fish, invertebrates, carrion, refuse. Often flocks with other gulls.

**Voice:** Typical for gull.

**Did you know?** Most of the "seagulls" found along the British Columbia coast nest on inland lakes far from the ocean.

**Date and Location Seen:** _____

Breeding

Non-breeding

First-year

**Description:** 58 cm, wingspan 140 cm. Medium-large gull; transitions to full adult plumage over four years. BREEDING: Underparts, tail white, grey back, **wingtips appear all-grey from below** but blackish with white tips from above. Round head, **dark eye** (pale in small percentage), **small bill** with red spot, **legs bright pink**. NON-BREEDING: Head heavily streaked. FIRST-YEAR: Variably mottled brown, darker wingtips edged white, bill black.

**Similar Species:** Dark wingtips of other gulls apparent from below as well as from above. Herring Gull (page 187) adult has yellow eye. Adult California Gull (page 185) has greenish-yellow legs. Hybrid Glaucous-winged × Western Gull (page 191) bill much heavier, forehead sloping.

**Seasonal Abundance:** Fairly common winter resident in region, arrives by October, departs March. Breeds in central Canadian Arctic; most winter along Pacific Coast, southeastern Alaska–Baja California.

**Where to Find:** Shorelines; good viewing at Clover Point, Victoria.

**Habitat:** Primarily coastal, especially estuaries. Also ponds, fields, lots.

**Diet and Behaviour:** Omnivorous. Forages mostly for fish, molluscs, carrion, urban refuse. Gregarious, often flocking with other gulls.

**Voice:** Typical for gull.

**Did you know?** Thayer's Gull, once classified as a race of Herring Gull, is now considered more closely related to Kumlien's (Iceland) Gull that breeds in the eastern Canadian Arctic.

**Date and Location Seen:** _____

Western Gull

Breeding

First-year

**Description:** 64 cm, wingspan 147 cm. Large gull; transitions to full adult plumage over four years. BREEDING: White head, underparts, tail, pearl-grey back; **wingtips same grey as back**, white spots near tip. **Massive yellow bill** with red spot near tip, **pink legs**. NON-BREEDING: Head streaked. FIRST-YEAR: Rather uniform brownish or greyish, including wingtips; bill black.

**Similar Species:** Most gulls smaller with smaller bills; other large gulls have black wingtips, except Glaucous Gull (not shown; rare in region), which has white wingtips.

**Seasonal Abundance:** Common resident in region. Ranges along Pacific Coast, Alaska to Mexico.

**Where to Find:** Primarily coastal, also fresh water throughout lowlands.

**Habitat:** Marine habitats; also lowland lakes, rivers, cities.

**Diet and Behaviour:** Omnivorous, opportunistic. Forages on land, water for fish, molluscs, carrion in coastal areas, refuse in cities, worms in fields. Nests in pairs on cliffs, pilings, roofs, other structures. Gregarious, flocking with other gulls.

**Voice:** Calls, typical for gull, include sequences of laugh-like bugling, staccato *ca ca ca* given in alarm.

**Did you know?** Glaucous-winged Gull hybridizes with the more southerly **Western Gull** (see inset; uncommon in region), which is **dark grey** above with **black wingtips**. The resulting offspring are intermediate in plumage. Many "Glaucous-wingeds" in southwestern British Columbia, especially in winter, are actually hybrids, with wingtips a shade darker than the back.

**Date and Location Seen:** _____

Breeding

**Description:** 51 cm, wingspan 122 cm. Stocky tern, white below, pearl-grey back with large, **thick red bill, black cap**, whitish, shallowly forked tail, **long, pointed wings** with dark tips on undersurface. NON-BREEDING: Whitish forehead. JUVENILE: Whitish forehead, back mottled with brown.

**Similar Species:** Common Tern (page 195), Arctic Tern (page 401) smaller, bill thin. Except for Heermann's (page 179), gulls lack red bill.

**Seasonal Abundance:** Fairly common summer resident in region (April–September). Ranges nearly worldwide in temperate, tropical zones.

**Where to Find:** Throughout lowlands, but local. Most easily seen on Fraser Delta, particularly Roberts Bank.

**Habitat:** Coastal habitats, rivers, lakes. Nests in isolated pairs or large colonies, uses open sites including recently disturbed ground, dredge-spoil islands, rooftops, undisturbed lots.

**Diet and Behaviour:** Forages fairly high over salt or fresh water, plunge-dives for small fish, often several feet below surface; also picks fish off surface. Carries fish in bill back to nest. Colony locations may shift year to year depending on disturbance.

**Voice:** Often heard before seen. Common call low, harsh, screeching *kaa yarrr*. Juveniles beg with whistled *wheee oo*.

**Did you know?** The Caspian Tern was first seen on the British Columbia coast in 1959, but has since become a locally common summer resident.

**Date and Location Seen:** _____

**Description:** 33 cm, wingspan 76 cm. **Slim, elegant**, white below with pearl-grey back, **black cap**, thin, black-tipped red bill, short, reddish legs. **Tail strongly forked**, white with dark edges; **wings long, pointed** with dark wedge at tip on upper surface. JUVENILE: Black bill, white forehead.

**Similar Species:** Bonaparte's Gull (page 177) has square tail, white stripe on forewing. Caspian Tern (page 193) much larger with thick bill. Arctic Tern (page 401) with shorter legs; breeding has all-red bill. Forster's Tern (not shown; rare in region) in breeding plumage has paler underparts, upperwing, dark-tipped orange bill; non-breeding with black mask, white on back of head.

**Seasonal Abundance:** Fairly common migrant, mostly late summer–fall. Ranges worldwide except Antarctica.

**Where to Find:** Locally on marine waters throughout region.

**Habitat:** Limited in region to coastal waters, although elsewhere also uses freshwater habitats. Often concentrates near tidal rips, roosts on beaches, piers, boats.

**Diet and Behaviour:** Forages for small fish by flying low over water, hovering, plunge-diving to catch prey with bill. Gregarious, often flocks with small gulls.

**Voice:** Calls include clipped *kip*, harsh but musical, slurred *kee ahrr*.

**Did you know?** Common Terns pass through British Columbia as they migrate from Prairie-province breeding grounds to oceanic waters off South America, where they winter.

**Date and Location Seen:** _____

Breeding

Non-breeding

**Description:** 41 cm, wingspan 69 cm. In all plumages, **back, crown blackish-brown, breast, underparts white, bill long, straight, black**. BREEDING: Entire head, throat dark (plumage held for much of winter). NON-BREEDING: White extends across throat, lower face to nape, with **dark line curving down behind eye**. IMMATURE: Resembles non-breeding adult.

**Similar Species:** Larger size, longer bill, solid blackish back, upperwing separate it from non-breeding Marbled, Ancient Murrelets (page 201), Pigeon Guillemot (page 199).

**Seasonal Abundance:** Fairly common winter resident on marine waters in region; abundance varies year to year. Nests on steep seaside cliffs in Arctic, temperate zones throughout northern hemisphere, including British Columbia outer coast. Most birds winter far offshore.

**Where to Find:** Good places include Active Pass, Discovery Passage. Breeds on Triangle Island off northern tip of Vancouver Island.

**Habitat:** Mostly open marine waters with strong tidal flow.

**Diet and Behaviour:** Dives for fish, squid, crustaceans. Congregates at good feeding sites.

**Voice:** Silent away from breeding colonies.

**Did you know?** Commons Murres routinely dive to 60 metres, propelling themselves with small wings adapted for underwater swimming. In the air, however, they must beat their wings in a rapid blur to keep their one-kilogram bodies aloft.

**Date and Location Seen:** _____

Breeding

Non-breeding

**Description:** 33 cm, wingspan 58 cm. Bill thin, straight, black; **legs, mouth lining vermilion-red**. BREEDING: **Mostly blackish-brown** except upper surface of forewing largely white—when wing folded, appears as l**arge white patch** with black slash on lower edge. NON-BREEDING: **Mostly white** with mottled back, dark line behind eye; white wing patch, dark wingtips retained. JUVENILE: Resembles non-breeding adult, but duskier.

**Similar Species:** In flight, much larger White-winged Scoter (page 65) shows white speculum (trailing edge of wing); Pigeon Guillemot's white patch is on forewing.

**Seasonal Abundance:** Fairly common year-round resident in region. Ranges along both coasts of North Pacific Ocean from Bering Strait south to California, Kurile Islands.

**Where to Find:** Widely distributed on marine waters; avoids brackish waters of Fraser Delta.

**Habitat:** Shallow, protected salt water, adjacent shoreline.

**Diet and Behaviour:** Takes small fish, shrimp, crabs, other organisms, at surface or by diving.

**Voice:** Trills, whistles given near nest.

**Did you know?** Pigeon Guillemots nest in varied coastal settings including hollows beneath projecting ledges and wooden platforms, crevices in rocky jetties and breakwaters, ferry dock girders, and burrows that they excavate in sandy bluffs.

**Date and Location Seen:** _____

**Breeding**

**Ancient Murrelet**

**Non-breeding**

**Description:** 25 cm, wingspan 41cm. Compact, short-necked alcid with **small, dark bill**. BREEDING: Brownish. Head, wings dark, **body "marbled" brown-and-buffy**. NON-BREEDING: Black upperparts, white flanks, **white streak where wings join back**. White chin, throat, collar give bird **black-capped look**. Wings narrower, more pointed than other alcids in region.

**Similar Species:** **Ancient Murrelet** (see inset; breeds British Columbia, Alaska, Siberia, small numbers present in region late fall–early winter). Same size as Marbled, with **yellow bill, grey back, no white streak** where wings join back. Black chin, nape, crown, less extensive white collar give bird **white-cheeked look. Underwing white** (dark in Marbled).

**Seasonal Abundance:** Uncommon year-round resident in region; in winter usually seen in pairs. Ranges Aleutians to California; populations seriously declining.

**Where to Find:** Relatively shallow saltwater bays, inlets, passages (Barkley Sound, Desolation Sound, Johnstone Strait, Sunshine Coast). Ancient Murrelet similarly distributed.

**Habitat:** Nests high in trees in forests away from coast, commuting to salt water to forage; winters on protected marine waters.

**Diet and Behaviour:** Dives for small fish, crustaceans, other sea animals. Flies with rapid wingbeats.

**Voice:** Flight call loud, high-pitched *keer keer keer* series, mostly near nest.

**Did you know?** The first Marbled Murrelet nest was discovered only in 1974.

**Date and Location Seen:** _____

Breeding

**Description:** 38 cm, wingspan 56 cm. Head, wings, body above water line **dark grey-brown**; light belly visible in flight. **Large yellow bill** (grey in juveniles). BREEDING: **White plumes** form streaks behind eye, bill; variable short "horn" at base of upper bill.

**Similar Species:** Marbled Murrelet (page 201) in breeding plumage much smaller, thin-billed, with darker belly. Tufted Puffin (page 401) similar in non-breeding, immature plumages, but much heavier with huge bill; dark belly visible in flight.

**Seasonal Abundance:** Common resident in region, April–September; uncommon winter resident. Breeds on many small islands along western, northern coasts of Vancouver Island; majority winter at sea. Ranges along both sides of Pacific from Aleutians south to Japan, California.

**Where to Find:** April–September, Clover Point in Victoria, Ogden Point, Johnstone Strait.

**Habitat:** Salt water, usually fairly deep (15 metres or more). Often forages in tide rips.

**Diet and Behaviour:** Dives for fish. Nests colonially, visiting nests only at night.

**Voice:** Mostly silent away from nests.

**Did you know?** Male and female "Rhinos" excavate nest burrows up to 4 metres deep in soil on grassy, brushy slopes well above the shoreline.

**Date and Location Seen:** _____

**Description:** 33 cm, wingspan 71 cm. Familiar domestic pigeon, **highly variable in colour, patterning**. Most common ("wild") form grey with **dark bill**, reddish legs, feet, dark head, neck; iridescent feathers on neck, two black bars across wing, **black band at tip of tail. White rump, underwing** visible in flight.

**Similar Species:** Band-tailed Pigeon (page 207) has yellow bill with black tip; grey, not white rump, white on nape of neck, broad grey band on tail, yellow legs, dark underwing.

**Seasonal Abundance:** Common, widespread year-round resident in region. Native to Old World; domesticated birds introduced, now naturalized essentially worldwide, continually augmented by escapes from captivity.

**Where to Find:** Cities, towns, rural settings near human habitation.

**Habitat:** City parks, streets, overpasses, industrial zones; rural seed fields, farms, grain elevators.

**Diet and Behaviour:** Forages mostly on ground for grain, seeds, grasses, food scraps. Feeds, travels in flocks. Nests on human-built structures. Intelligent, adaptable; raised since antiquity for show or as table delicacy. Captive breeding responsible for wide variety of plumages found among naturalized populations.

**Voice:** Soft cooing.

**Did you know?** Fast flyers with superb homing instincts, Rock Pigeons have been selectively bred for speed and endurance and trained for racing. Champion racers may fly at average speeds of 150 kilometres per hour over a 600-kilometre course.

**Date and Location Seen:** _____

**Description:** 36 cm, wingspan 66 cm. Overall grey with purplish head, breast, **black-tipped yellow bill, grey rump, pale grey band on tail, yellow legs**, white bar above iridescent feathers on nape (absent in juveniles). **Dark underwing** visible in flight.

**Similar Species:** Rock Pigeon (page 205) has white, not grey, rump, reddish legs, all-dark bill, white underwing.

**Seasonal Abundance:** Fairly common summer resident in region, uncommon in winter; most go south September–October, return beginning late February. Ranges from southwestern British Columbia, Colorado, to Argentina.

**Where to Find:** Well-treed neighbourhoods, parks, marine shorelines, foothills..

**Habitat:** Breeds in low-elevation coniferous, mixed forests; uncommon to mountain passes. Prefers tall conifers, forest edges with nearby open spaces. Post-breeders, migrants regular in mountains.

**Diet and Behaviour:** Feeds mostly on nuts, seeds, fruits of deciduous trees, shrubs such as oak, cherry, elderberry, arbutus, cascara. Attracted to feeders with black-oil sunflower, cracked corn, millet. Usually forages, travels in small flocks. When taking flight, wings produce loud clapping noise.

**Voice:** Low, repetitive *whoo oo whoo.*

**Did you know?** Garry-oak acorns and arbutus berries are two favourite winter foods for Band-tailed Pigeons. The small winter populations of this bird in British Columbia are concentrated at sites with one or both of these trees.

**Date and Location Seen:** _____

**Description:** 30 cm, wingspan 46 cm. **Slender**; mostly tan-coloured with **long, pointed tail**, black spots on pointed wings, reddish legs. Male has pinkish hue to breast, blue crown. **Bill small, thin, black**. White tips of outer tail feathers visible in flight.

**Similar Species:** Band-tailed Pigeon (page 207), Rock Pigeon (page 205) grey, considerably heavier-bodied, tail proportionally shorter.

**Seasonal Abundance:** Uncommon, local year-round resident in Fraser Valley, rare on southern Vancouver Island. Some migrate south for winter. Ranges from southern Canada to Panama.

**Where to Find:** Fraser Valley, Delta, Saanich farm fields.

**Habitat:** Lowlands. Mostly open habitats including grasslands (prairie, agricultural), recent clear-cuts, semi-rural residential tracts, towns. Attracted to feeders.

**Diet and Behaviour:** Eats mostly seeds, grains (sunflower seed, millet, cracked corn at feeders). Often seen on overhead wires. Picks up gravel along railroad tracks, roadsides to help grind its food. In winter, forms flocks at sites with plentiful food, nearby trees for sheltering, roosting. When taking flight, wings whistle.

**Voice:** Slow, mournful cooing, *ooo aaa ooo ooo ooo*.

**Did you know?** The Passenger Pigeon, driven to extinction in the 19th century, was once the most widespread, common, and prolific member of the pigeon/dove family in North America—a distinction now held by its close relative, the Mourning Dove.

**Date and Location Seen:** _____

**Description:** 38 cm, wingspan 102 cm. **Slim, long-legged, round-headed** owl with prominent **heart-shaped facial disc**, dark brown eyes, long, yellowish, hooked bill. Brownish-tan back with pearl-grey spots, mostly white underparts, impart **pale appearance**. In flight, tail looks fairly long, wings appear bowed.

**Similar Species:** Barred Owl (page 221) bulkier, broader-winged. Short-eared Owl (page 223) has floppier flight, dark wing patches.

**Seasonal Abundance:** Fairly common resident in region, but local. Ranges worldwide in temperate, tropical zones.

**Where to Find:** Fraser Delta, southeastern Vancouver Island.

**Habitat:** Open areas: farm fields, wetlands, urban landscapes.

**Diet and Behaviour:** Extremely nocturnal. Hunts from perches or in low flight by sight, sound, captures prey in talons. Directional hearing well developed for locating meadow mice, its primary quarry, in high grass. Also takes some birds, insects, frogs. Roosts in buildings or dense conifers by day. Like all owls, does not build nest. Lays up to 10 eggs in dark corner of building, large nest box, cave, tree cavity.

**Voice:** Varied calls include harsh, grating screech, long hiss, series of metallic clicks.

**Did you know?** Townsend's vole, the common meadow mouse of coastal British Columbia, makes up about 98 percent of the Barn Owl diet in this region.

**Date and Location Seen:** _____

**Description:** 19 cm. **Small** but robust, mottled greyish or brownish, **block-headed** with **prominent ear tufts** (sometimes held flat), **yellow eyes**. Breast, belly streaked, finely barred.

**Similar Species:** Combination of small size, ear tufts, yellow eyes eliminates other owls.

**Seasonal Abundance:** Uncommon to locally fairly common resident in region. Ranges across western North America from southeastern Alaska to Mexico.

**Where to Find:** Local; often absent in suitable-looking habitat. Mostly lowlands, river drainages up to moderate elevation.

**Habitat:** Broadleaf, mixed woodlands, including forest edge, parks, backyards. Often along watercourses.

**Diet and Behaviour:** Extremely nocturnal. Hunts from perches, swoops, captures prey in talons. Locates prey by sight, sound. Favours rodents, large insects, but will take birds, reptiles, amphibians, fish, slugs, worms. Like all owls, does not build nest; uses existing tree cavities. Usually responds to imitations of its calls by approaching, calling to protect territory.

**Voice:** Common call accelerating series of low whistles in pattern of ball bouncing; also double trill.

**Did you know?** Western Screech-Owl populations in Vancouver and Victoria have declined sharply over the last 20 years, probably due to direct predation by newly arrived Barred Owls.

**Date and Location Seen:** _____

**Description:** 56 cm, wingspan 114 cm. Formidable owl, mottled greyish-brown, **block-headed** with **prominent ear tufts. Yellow eyes**, brownish facial disc, **white throat**, finely barred lower breast, belly.

**Similar Species:** Long-eared Owl (not shown; rare in region) also has prominent ear tufts, but smaller (38 cm, one-fifth as heavy) with vertical streaks below.

**Seasonal Abundance:** Fairly common resident in countryside in region, somewhat less common in cities (may increase with influx of fall transients). Ranges throughout New World, from Arctic to South America.

**Where to Find:** Lowlands to treeline, although uncommon in dense coniferous forest.

**Habitat:** Adaptable. Woodlands, meadows, farmlands, city parks.

**Diet and Behaviour:** Hunts mostly at night, watching, listening for prey from perch, then capturing it with talons. Diet extremely varied, mostly medium-sized mammals but also birds, large insects, cold-blooded animals including fish. Like all owls, does not build nest; uses snags, cavities, stick nests of other species, especially Red-tailed Hawk. One of earliest nesting birds, lays eggs as early as January.

**Voice:** Common call deep *whoo whodoo whoo who*. Begging young give harsh shrieks.

**Did you know?** Great Horned Owls are powerful hunters, taking prey such as rabbits, skunks, muskrats, grouse, and cats.

**Date and Location Seen:** _____

**Description:** 56 cm, wingspan 127 cm. **Round-headed, yellow-eyed, mostly white**, varying amounts of dark mottling. Adult male may be pure white; female, immature may have dense, dark barring.

**Similar Species:** None in region.

**Seasonal Abundance:** Only a few individuals present in region most years. Periodically irrupts southward (November–early April) due to high reproduction, subsequent food shortage in Arctic where nests, normally winters. Ranges around northern hemisphere in tundra belt.

**Where to Find:** When present, concentrates in open coastal habitats. Best bets Fraser Delta, Boundary Bay dykes.

**Habitat:** Agricultural fields, beaches, intertidal zone, salt marshes, estuaries, urban areas.

**Diet and Behaviour:** Hunts mostly at dusk, dawn but takes prey any time. Sits on ground, other low perches, structures; takes flight, captures prey with talons. Often concentrates in loose groups near flocks of waterfowl (important food source in region).

**Voice:** Almost entirely silent in winter. Screams, hoots on tundra.

**Did you know?** The biggest recorded incursion of Snowy Owls into British Columbia occurred in the winter of 1973–1974, when 107 were seen on the Ladner Christmas Bird Count—still a North American record.

**Date and Location Seen:** _____

**Description:** 17 cm. **Tiny** greyish-brown owl with **no ear tufts**, small facial disk, yellow eyes, **long tail**.

**Similar Species:** Small size, daytime activity pattern unique among owls in region. Northern Saw-whet Owl (page 225) larger, browner, with much larger head, shorter tail.

**Seasonal Abundance:** Uncommon year-round resident in region. Ranges from Rockies westward, southern British Columbia to Honduras.

**Where to Find:** Coniferous forests throughout region; Manning Provincial Park, Cypress Provincial Park, Maplewood Conservation Area, Pacific Rim National Park good sites.

**Habitat:** Open coniferous forests at low-to-middle elevations; sometimes seen at forest edge in suburban areas in winter.

**Diet and Behaviour:** Hunts during day for mice, small birds. Nests in old woodpecker cavities, such as those made by Hairy Woodpeckers.

**Voice:** Long, slow (one note every two seconds) series of hollow, whistled *kook* notes, accelerating into rapid trill when agitated.

**Did you know?** Small birds mob pygmy-owls when they hear one call, flying toward the owl, vocalizing noisily. This is a learned response, so if you imitate a pygmy-owl's call and provoke a strong reaction from local chickadees and nuthatches, you are likely in a pygmy-owl territory.

**Date and Location Seen:** _____

**Description:** 48 cm, wingspan 107 cm. Bulky, greyish, with **dark brown eyes. Rounded head** with white lines in ring-like pattern above dark-bordered facial disc. Hooked bill yellowish, upperparts mottled, streaked. **Upper breast barred; lower breast, belly whitish with dark streaks**.

**Similar Species:** Great Horned Owl (page 215) has ear tufts, yellow eyes. Barn Owl (page 211) slimmer. Spotted Owl (not shown; rare, vanishing resident of old-growth forests in region) dark brown, lacks streaks below.

**Seasonal Abundance:** Recent arrival in region, now fairly common resident. Ranges across southern Canada, throughout eastern, northwestern U.S.

**Where to Find:** Throughout region including forested parks within cities.

**Habitat:** Wet mixed, broadleaf forests; prefers dense woods but may disperse in fall to more urbanized settings.

**Diet and Behaviour:** Mostly nocturnal. Hunts from perches; favours rodents, but eats other small mammals, birds, reptiles, amphibians, large insects. Like all owls, does not build nest—uses large cavities, nests of other species. Vocal, territorial, occasionally even toward humans.

**Voice:** Loud hoots including *who cooks for you, who cooks for you allll* sequence.

**Did you know?** Barred Owls first reached British Columbia in the 1940s in the northern part of the province, and arrived in southwestern British Columbia toward 1970.

**Date and Location Seen:** _____

**Description:** 36 cm, wingspan 97 cm. **Moth-like flight** on long wings. Streaked upperparts, upper breast, light below. In flight shows **dark patch near wrist**, buff patch toward outer end of upperwing. Yellow eyes, prominent facial disc; short ear tufts seldom visible.

**Similar Species:** Slow, floppy flight, daytime activity unlike other large owls in region.

**Seasonal Abundance:** Fairly common migrant, winter resident in region (October–April); rare breeder. Ranges through much of northern hemisphere, vacating northern parts in winter; also resident in South America.

**Where to Find:** Quite local in open habitat. Most common on Fraser Delta, around Boundary Bay.

**Habitat:** Open, wet meadows, fallow agricultural fields, coastal marshes.

**Diet and Behaviour:** Highly migratory, nomadic. Hunts low over fields, mostly near dawn, dusk, but may fly at night or in full daylight. Locates voles, other small mammals, birds by sight, sound, often hovering before pouncing, capturing with talons. Concentrates in loose flocks at areas of prey abundance, roosts on ground by day.

**Voice:** Gives nasal barks, wheezy whistles when multiple birds hunt.

**Did you know?** Short-eared Owls nest on the ground. As many as 10 young may leave a nest in as little as two weeks.

**Date and Location Seen:** _____

Juvenile

**Description:** 18 cm. Small owl with large, **round head, yellow eyes**; white below with broad, brown streaking, brown back, large white wing spots, **fine white streaks on face, head**. JUVENILE: Plain brown, ochre below, with white forehead.

**Similar Species:** Western Screech-Owl (page 213) larger, block-headed, with ear tufts (although these may be held flat). Northern Pygmy-Owl (page 219) smaller, with long tail, smaller head, typically active in daylight. Boreal Owl (not shown; limited to high mountains) rather similar but considerably larger.

**Seasonal Abundance:** Fairly common resident in region but seldom seen, numbers augmented in winter by migrants. Ranges across North America from southeastern Alaska to eastern Maritimes, south in mountains to Mexico.

**Where to Find:** Widespread. A few may winter at Reifel Sanctuary.

**Habitat:** Coniferous, mixed woodlands at all elevations.

**Diet and Behaviour:** Extremely nocturnal. Locates prey by sight, sound; favours rodents, also takes birds, insects. Nests in tree cavities, habitually roosts in winter in one spot in dense conifers where best located by resulting pile of pellets, whitewash. Somewhat migratory; may move south or downslope in fall.

**Voice:** Calls including rhythmic tooting, *skew* notes, twitters, barks, whining whistles, may be elicited by imitation of its tooting call.

**Did you know?** Migrating Northern Saw-whet Owls concentrate in fall at Rocky Point west of Victoria. Researchers there have banded over 400 individuals in one season.

**Date and Location Seen:** _____

**Description:** 24 cm, wingspan 61 cm. Short-legged, relatively long-tailed, **mottled greyish-brown** above, banded brown below; **long, pointed, angular wings with conspicuous broad white band near tip. Usually seen high in flight**. Appears owl-like at rest; wingtips extend beyond tail tip. MALE: White chin, tail band. FEMALE: Buffy chin.

**Similar Species:** Swallows, swifts much smaller; falcons have more direct flight, lack white wing bands.

**Seasonal Abundance:** Uncommon migrant, summer resident in region (late May–early September). Highly migratory; breeds across most of North, Middle America, winters South America.

**Where to Find:** Throughout region. Most often seen on eastern Vancouver Island, Sunshine Coast; essentially absent from Greater Vancouver.

**Habitat:** Open habitats: forest clearings, stony ground, weedy lots. Hunts, migrates over cities, forests, fields.

**Diet and Behaviour:** Forages aerially with erratic flight—mostly near dawn, dusk, but active at any hour. Short bill opens to huge gape for catching insects. Perches lengthwise along branches. Nests on open ground, relying on camouflage.

**Voice:** Far-carrying nasal buzz given repeatedly in flight.

**Did you know?** Male Common Nighthawks display over their territories by opening their wings at the bottom of shallow dives, making a loud *vooom* as the air vibrates the wing feathers.

**Date and Location Seen:** _____

**Black Swift**

**Vaux's Swift**

**Description:** BLACK largest North American swift (18.5 cm, 45 g), VAUX'S smallest (12 cm, 20 g). Both darkish overall, usually seen foraging high overhead on **pointed, curving wings** with **flickering wingbeats**. BLACK: Broader wingbase, **longer tail (often notched). Wingbeat slower**, shallower; glides frequently. VAUX'S: **Throat, breast, rump paler** than rest of plumage (hard to spot in field); short tail tapers to point when closed, giving **"winged cigar"** look. **Wingbeat rapid** with only brief intervals of gliding.

**Similar Species:** Swallows may use similar aerial foraging strategy, but wingbeats not so flickering; wings proportionally shorter, broader, less swept back.

**Seasonal Abundance:** Summer residents in region, locally fairly common. Return May, depart August–September. Main nesting ranges southeastern Alaska to Central America; winter from Mexico to South America.

**Where to Find:** Manning Park, Cypress Park, many other sites.

**Habitat:** BLACK: Nests in mountains, forages in lowlands when clouds envelop mountains. VAUX'S: Nests widely in hollow cedars, cottonwoods (occasionally chimneys). Both hunt opportunistically, often over wetlands, lakes, streams.

**Diet and Behaviour:** Small insects taken on wing.

**Voice:** Chip notes. BLACK often in series; VAUX'S rapid, higher-pitched, hummingbird-like.

**Did you know?** Black Swifts nest behind high waterfalls or in narrow, moist canyons. Vaux's Swifts roost communally in smokestacks, belfries, and hollow trees in fall migration.

**Date and Location Seen:** _____

Male

Female

**Description:** 10 cm. MALE: Green back, greyish underparts, **iridescent red crown**, throat (can appear black in shadow), dark tail. FEMALE: Similar except outer tail feathers tipped white, red restricted to small spot on throat. IMMATURE: Little or no red.

**Similar Species:** Female/immature Rufous Hummingbirds (page 233) have rufous flanks, tail base, undertail.

**Seasonal Abundance:** Locally common year-round resident in region. Original range along Pacific Coast from northern Baja California to San Francisco Bay; now breeds north to Vancouver Island, east to Arizona.

**Where to Find:** Southern Vancouver Island, Greater Vancouver; uncommon elsewhere.

**Habitat:** Human-influenced: parks, gardens, residential neighbourhoods. Hummingbird feeders, exotic flowering plants may help account for phenomenally successful range extension.

**Diet and Behaviour:** Consumes flower nectar, sugar water from hummingbird feeders, tree sap (often from holes drilled by sapsuckers), small insects, spiders. Can survive short bouts of severe cold weather by converting more sugar to fat or by lowering body temperature to enter torpor (dormancy).

**Voice:** Loud chip note. Song dry, rasping, delivered year round from exposed perch. Various squeaks, buzzes, chattering sounds in courtship, territorial defence.

**Did you know?** Male Anna's defend their territories with "dive displays," looping 15–35 metres into the air then zooming down to emit a loud pop in the intruder's face.

**Date and Location Seen:** _____

Male

Female

**Description:** 9.5 cm. Bill straight, dark. MALE: **Back, tail, underparts rusty-orange**; back may have variable amounts of green. Crown green, upper breast white, throat iridescent orange-red. FEMALE: Upperparts, crown green; **tail base, undertail, flanks rufous**; outer tail feathers white-tipped. Red feathering on throat varies from none up to small spot. IMMATURE: Resembles female.

**Similar Species:** Female/immature Anna's Hummingbirds (page 231) show no rufous coloration.

**Seasonal Abundance:** Common summer resident in region. Breeds from northern California to southern Alaska, western Alberta; winters in southern U.S., Mexico. Males arrive before females in spring, usually in early March; adults leave coast in early July, young in August.

**Where to Find:** Widespread.

**Habitat:** Forest openings, disturbed areas, brushy edges; lowlands in spring, moves up into flowering meadows in mountains as season progresses.

**Diet and Behaviour:** Consumes nectar from flowers, sugar water from hummingbird feeders, sap from holes in trees, small insects, spiders. Male has diving, J-shaped courtship display.

**Voice:** Chip, other warning notes. No song. Adult male's wings make high-pitched trilling.

**Did you know?** Rufous Hummingbird is the northernmost representative of this largely tropical New World family. The first northbound migrants arrive in southwestern British Columbia in early March, following the blossoming of salmonberry and red-flowering currant.

**Date and Location Seen:** _____

233

**Male**

**Female**

**Description:** 33 cm. **Large head, unkempt crest, stout bill.** MALE: Mostly slate-blue with **white underparts**, collar; wide **slate-blue breastband**. FEMALE: Identical but with rufous flanks, additional rufous band across lower breast. JUVENILE: Single dark breast band, rufous flanks.

**Similar Species:** None in region.

**Seasonal Abundance:** Common year-round resident in region. Nests continent wide—below Arctic tundra, north of arid Southwest. Retreats from northernmost parts at freeze-up; winters along Pacific Coast (Aleutians south), across most of U.S., throughout Mexico, Caribbean (a few farther south).

**Where to Find:** From sea level to subalpine, any stretch of shore with good nest sites, fishing prospects has its pair of kingfishers.

**Habitat:** Along streams, lakes, ponds, saltwater shorelines with clear, relatively still waters where it can see prey.

**Diet and Behaviour:** Watches from perch over water, or hovers; plunges in shallow dive (less than 60 centimetres below surface), seizes prey in bill. Takes mostly fish, some insects, crustaceans, other animals. Digs nest burrows, usually one to two metres deep in banks.

**Voice:** Main call loud rattle, somewhat like sound of ratchet noisemaker toy, given all year (often in flight).

**Did you know?** A Belted Kingfisher returns to its perch with a freshly caught fish in its bill, beats it senseless against the perch, then swallows it headfirst.

**Date and Location Seen:** _____

Juvenile

**Description:** 22 cm. Typical woodpecker tree-clinging behaviour, undulating flight, chisel-like bill. Colourful. Breast, **head entirely red** except for faint white moustache mark; belly yellowish, back black with white mottling. Elongated **white patch across center of upperwing**. JUVENILE: Dark brownish, moults to adult plumage by September.

**Similar Species:** Red-naped Sapsucker (not shown; rare in region except at crest of Cascade, Coast mountains) has white facial lines, no red below throat. Pileated Woodpecker (page 245) larger, crested; white patch closer to end of wing.

**Seasonal Abundance:** Fairly common resident in region. Ranges down coast, southeastern Alaska to Baja California.

**Where to Find:** Coniferous, mixed forests; in winter may use urban parks, backyards, small woodlots.

**Habitat:** Prefers cedar-hemlock-spruce-dominated forests, but also found in various mixed woods.

**Diet and Behaviour:** Quietly drills evenly spaced small holes in live trees, revisiting these "wells" on regular foraging routes to drink sap, feed on insects attracted to sap, berries, tree tissues. Moves downslope below level of heavy snow in winter. Excavates nest hole in coniferous snag, aspen, or other soft wood.

**Voice:** Nasal mews, squeals; territorial drumming irregularly spaced.

**Did you know?** Red-breasted Sapsucker interbreeds with the closely related Red-naped Sapsucker at the crest of the Coast and Cascade mountains, resulting in intermediate-plumaged hybrids.

**Date and Location Seen:** _____

Male

Female

**Description:** 17 cm. **Short, chisel-like bill**, stiff tail, tree-clinging behaviour. **Dingy white or buffy back**, underparts, eyebrow, moustache mark; black bars on white outer tail feathers; **wings checkered black-and-white**. MALE: Red spot at back of head. JUVENILE: Red on top of head.

**Similar Species:** Hairy Woodpecker (page 241) identical but larger, with bill as long as distance from back of head to bill base (Downy's bill only half this measurement).

**Seasonal Abundance:** Common lowland resident in region, becoming uncommon at higher elevations. Ranges from Alaska to Labrador, south to Florida, Texas, California.

**Where to Find:** Woodlands, parks, neighbourhoods, stream corridors, semi-open rural habitats, mostly at low elevations.

**Habitat:** Prefers broadleaf woods, but also found in mixed forests, hedgerows, gardens.

**Diet and Behaviour:** Probes dead limbs, small twigs, weed stalks in search of insects, also feeds on fruits, seeds. Excavates nest cavity in dead wood; calls, drums to establish territory. Common at suet feeders. Flight undulating, like that of other woodpeckers.

**Voice:** Calls include rattle-like whinny, flat *pik* (not as sharp as that given by Hairy Woodpecker).

**Did you know?** Male and female Downy Woodpeckers often maintain separate feeding territories in winter.

**Date and Location Seen:** _____

Male

Female

**Description:** 23 cm. **Long chisel-like bill**, stiff tail, tree-clinging behaviour. **Dingy white back**, underparts, eyebrow, moustache mark, outer tail feathers; **wings checkered black-and-white**. MALE: Red spot at back of head. JUVENILE: Red on top of head.

**Similar Species:** Downy Woodpecker (page 239) identical but smaller, shorter-billed, with black spots on outer tail (juvenile Hairy may also show these).

**Seasonal Abundance:** Fairly common resident in region. Ranges from Alaska to Labrador, south to Central America, Caribbean.

**Where to Find:** Throughout region although scarce in urban areas.

**Habitat:** Prefers coniferous forest, but also uses mixed, broadleaf woods.

**Diet and Behaviour:** Excavates dead wood, scrapes bark, probes in search of insects; may also feed on fruits, seeds, sap. Digs nest cavities in live or dead wood; drums, calls to establish territory. Regular at bird feeders. Flight undulating, like that of other woodpeckers.

**Voice:** Calls include *pik krrreeeeer*, very sharp *piik* (louder than similar call given by Downy Woodpecker).

**Did you know?** Hairy and Downy Woodpeckers resident west of the Cascade and Coast mountains are dingy white. In winter, small numbers of bright white birds descend from the interior to coastal lowlands.

**Date and Location Seen:** _____

241

Red-shafted
Male

Yellow-shafted
Male

Red-shafted
Female

**Description:** 30 cm. Robust, colourful, with **black crescent bib, white rump**. Long bill, stiff tail, tree-clinging behaviour. Barred brown above, spotted buff below, with **brightly coloured feather shafts**, most notable in wings. Two forms. RED-SHAFTED: Brown cap, grey face, **red shafts**, male with red moustache mark. YELLOW-SHAFTED: Grey cap, brown face, **yellow shafts, red crescent on nape**, male with black moustache mark.

**Similar Species:** Distinctive in region.

**Seasonal Abundance:** Common resident in region but highly migratory. Ranges throughout North America, Middle America, Caribbean. Yellow-shafted, Red-shafted forms interbreed where ranges overlap in central British Columbia.

**Where to Find:** Throughout region.

**Habitat:** Open woodlands, any semi-open area, urban woodlots, lawns.

**Diet and Behaviour:** Forages on ground for ants, in trees for fruits, occasionally seeds. Boisterous interactions, loud calling, territorial drumming (sometimes on gutters, chimney flashing) make it noticeable. Excavates cavity nest in live or dead wood. Flight undulating, like that of other woodpeckers. Flocks in migration.

**Voice:** Calls include *woika woika woika*, long series of repeated *kuk* notes, piercing *keeww*.

**Did you know?** The red-shafted form resides year round in the region. Yellow-shafted birds are present fall to spring along with intergrades that show mixed characteristics.

**Date and Location Seen:** _____

# PILEATED WOODPECKER
## *Dryocopus pileatus*

**Description:** 41 cm. Chisel-like bill, stiff tail, tree-clinging behaviour, undulating flight typical of woodpeckers. **Large**, lanky; **black** except for **large crimson crest, white neck stripe**, facial markings, underwings, wing patch. MALE: Red moustache mark.

**Similar Species:** Much larger than other woodpeckers in region. Red, white markings, undulating flight distinguish it from crows.

**Seasonal Abundance:** Fairly common resident in region. Ranges across southern Canada, U.S., except for most of interior West.

**Where to Find:** Throughout region, including forest tracts, parks within urban areas.

**Habitat:** Mature coniferous, mixed forests.

**Diet and Behaviour:** Excavates large, deep, oval or rectangular holes in trees in search of insects, primarily ants. Chisels through hard wood to access insect-damaged tree centers. Also feeds on small fruits. Sometimes loud, obvious with tapping, banging, calling, but also secretive, hiding behind tree trunks. Often calls while flying above or within canopy.

**Voice:** Series of 10–15 wild-sounding *kuk* notes with irregular rhythm, abrupt ending. Territorial drumming slow, loud.

**Did you know?** With the exception of the almost extinct Ivory-billed Woodpecker of the southeastern United States and Cuba, the Pileated Woodpecker is the largest member of the woodpecker family north of Mexico.

**Date and Location Seen:** _____

**Description:** 19 cm. **Upright stance**, dark greyish-olive above, below, with wide white line extending from throat down chest to belly giving **vested appearance. Large head** with slight crest, long, dark bill, **short tail**, impart stout profile. White rump tufts seldom visible.

**Similar Species:** Western Wood-Pewee (page 249) smaller, appears less vested, with smaller bill.

**Seasonal Abundance:** Fairly common May–September resident in region, with migration, dispersal continuing throughout summer. Breeds from Alaska to Labrador, south in western mountains to New Mexico; winters to South America.

**Where to Find:** Throughout region, most common in mountains.

**Habitat:** Fairly mature coniferous forest; prefers tree stands interspersed with open areas, including clear-cuts, old burns, bogs, neighbourhoods, parks.

**Diet and Behaviour:** Makes wide-ranging sallies for large flying insects from exposed perch at top of tree or snag. Usually returns to perch in same spot. Calls frequently; best located by voice.

**Voice:** Song whistled *quick three beers* with second syllable strongly accented. Calls include *pep pep pep* repeated at short intervals.

**Did you know?** The Olive-sided Flycatcher is declining in numbers, especially in the East. Suggested causes include tropical habitat loss and a reduction in prey availability.

**Date and Location Seen:** _____

**Description:** 15 cm. **Upright stance**, dark olive-grey above, long wings with light-coloured **wing-bars, dusky chest**, pale yellowish belly. Slim with **fairly prominent crest**, dark bill with lighter base, **no eye-ring**.

**Similar Species:** More crested, but easily confused with smaller, lighter *Empidonax* flycatchers (pages 251–255). Olive-sided Flycatcher (page 247) larger with shorter tail, larger head, more vested appearance.

**Seasonal Abundance:** Fairly common resident in region from mid-May to mid-September. Breeds in West from Alaska south in mountains to Honduras, winters in South America.

**Where to Find:** Mostly lowlands but occurs to mountain passes. Seldom nests within urban areas but widespread in migration.

**Habitat:** Open woodlands, woodland edge, preferring broadleaf growth along water courses.

**Diet and Behaviour:** Forages from exposed perch in tall shrub or tree, making sallies to capture insects; may return to same spot. Often flutters wings while perching. Calls throughout day in spring, early summer, so best located by voice.

**Voice:** Most frequent call burry, nasal *prreeer*. Song, given at dawn, combination of tones similar to call.

**Did you know?** Western Wood-Pewees build their nests on the horizontal surface of limbs, usually at a fork.

**Date and Location Seen:** _____

**Description:** 14 cm. Fairly distinctive member of look-alike *Empidonax* flycatcher group. **Upright stance**; olive-brown above, buff-white wing-bars, whitish underparts. **Appears slim**, fairly long, with **long, broad, pale bill. Eye-ring minimal or absent**.

**Similar Species:** Other *Empidonax* flycatchers in region have prominent eye-rings. Western Wood-Pewee (page 249) slightly larger, much darker overall with more crested appearance.

**Seasonal Abundance:** Common resident in region mid-May to September. Ranges across continent from extreme southern Canada south to California, Georgia; winters from Mexico to Panama.

**Where to Find:** Mostly at lower elevation, but also up to mountain passes in clear-cuts. Nests within urban areas in appropriate habitat, scarce in migration away from nesting locations.

**Habitat:** Open, shrubby, wetland habitats, clear-cuts, brushy forest edge.

**Diet and Behaviour:** Forages from perch usually within tall shrub, making sallies to capture insects. Eats some berries in summer, fall. Easily located by voice: distinctive song given throughout day, but especially near dawn.

**Voice:** Harsh *fitz bew* song, with first syllable strongly accented. Calls include clear *whit*, buzzy *breet*.

**Did you know?** Identification of *Empidonax* flycatchers is notoriously difficult. The Alder Flycatcher—a close relative of the Willow Flycatcher that breeds farther north—is so similar that the two can be told apart only by their vocalizations.

**Date and Location Seen:** _____

**Description:** 13 cm. Difficult-to-identify member of look-alike *Empidonax* flycatcher group. **Upright stance; appears dark, large-headed**, long-winged. Greyish-green with wing-bars, yellowish wash on belly, **dusky grey chest**, grey head with distinct eye-ring. Short bill may appear all-dark.

**Similar Species:** Pacific-slope Flycatcher (page 255) slimmer, brighter, with more asymmetrical eye-ring. Willow Flycatcher (page 251) without eye-ring. Other *Empidonax* species rare in region (not shown). Western Wood-Pewee (page 249) larger, no eye-ring.

**Seasonal Abundance:** Common resident in region, mid-April to September. Breeds in West, Alaska to New Mexico; winters in highlands from southeastern Arizona to Honduras.

**Where to Find:** Nests in coniferous, mixed forests throughout region; most easily found from middle elevations to mountain passes. Widespread in migration.

**Habitat:** Prefers dense coniferous forests but also uses mixed woods, broadleaf thickets in migration.

**Diet and Behaviour:** Forages from perch, making sallies to capture insect prey. Often flicks tail, wings nervously. Feeds at all levels, but often remains high in dense coniferous growth.

**Voice:** Song consists of several phrases including burry, distinctive *bureek*. Calls include sharp *peet*.

**Did you know?** Hammond's Flycatchers can appear brightly coloured in fall—they moult into fresh plumage before migrating.

**Date and Location Seen:** _____

**Description:** 13 cm. Fairly distinctive member of look-alike *Empidonax* flycatcher group. **Upright stance**; olive-green with wing-bars; yellow wash on underparts extends up to throat. Wide, **pale bill, slightly crested appearance**; strong, **asymmetrical eye-ring**, elongated behind eye.

**Similar Species:** Other *Empidonax* flycatchers in region less yellow on upper breast, throat, with less prominent, more symmetrical eye-ring. Smaller, lighter-coloured than Western Wood-Pewee (page 249).

**Seasonal Abundance:** Common resident in region, mid-April to September. Breeds from southeastern Alaska south through British Columbia, Pacific states, to Baja California, winters in Mexico.

**Where to Find:** Nests throughout region from lowlands to mountain passes, including smaller wooded tracts within urban areas. Migrants also use thickets in parks, neighbourhoods.

**Habitat:** Shaded interior of moist, mixed or coniferous forests, preferably with broadleaf understory.

**Diet and Behaviour:** Forages by watching for insects while perched within leafy growth, then sallies to capture prey; stays close to cover. Difficult to see, but easily located by distinctive call. May eat some berries, especially in late summer.

**Voice:** High-pitched, rising, slurred *suweeet* call; three-part song of thin, squeaky notes heard less frequently.

**Did you know?** Pacific-slope Flycatchers build elegant moss nests on banks, rock bluffs, or large stumps.

**Date and Location Seen:** _____

Immature

**Description:** 24 cm. Large-headed, long-tailed songbird, mostly pearl-grey; **wings, tail, mask black. White marks** in wing, outer tail visible in flight. **Bill large** with slight hook. Immature browner, dark markings less distinct; scaling below.

**Similar Species:** Loggerhead Shrike (not shown; extremely rare in region) smaller with heavier mask that crosses over base of its smaller bill.

**Seasonal Abundance:** Uncommon resident in region, October to early April. Breeds on tundra around northern hemisphere, winters to temperate zone.

**Where to Find:** Lowlands to lower foothills; migrants may appear in open areas within cities. Good locations include Iona Island, Boundary Bay, Island View Beach, Cowichan Bay.

**Habitat:** Fields, coastal marshes, other open places with scattered trees, bushes.

**Diet and Behaviour:** Preys on small mammals, birds, insects by perching prominently, often at highest point of shrub, then swooping down, dispatching victim with bill. Often impales food on thorn or barbed wire in sheltered location to facilitate feeding or store for later use. Flight slightly undulating with rapid flapping, halting pauses.

**Voice:** Occasionally offers mellow, warbled phrases of song in winter quarters.

**Did you know?** Northern Shrikes, often called "butcher birds," appear in variable numbers each winter dependent on reproductive success and food supply in the far north.

**Date and Location Seen:** _____

**Description:** 14 cm. Compact with short tail, heavy bill. Greyish-green above with **greyer head**, white below with yellowish flanks. Prominent **white wing-bars, bold well-defined white spectacles**.

**Similar Species:** Hutton's Vireo (page 261) smaller with diffuse white eye-ring. Other vireos lack wing-bars. Red-eyed Vireo (page 265) song somewhat similar but more rapid with complex phrases.

**Seasonal Abundance:** Uncommon resident in region mid-April to September. Ranges in West from British Columbia to California, winters Mexico.

**Where to Find:** Well-treed lowlands throughout region. Good bets include Mount Tolmie, Minnekhada Park, Pacific Spirit Park. Migrants widespread anywhere with trees.

**Habitat:** Forests, especially Douglas-fir forests of eastern Vancouver Island, mixed forests in Fraser Valley. Migrants use woodland edge, parks, neighbourhoods.

**Diet and Behaviour:** Forages sluggishly, deliberately in upper canopy for insects, some small fruits. Inconspicuous unless singing; may sing less frequently than other vireos. Joins mixed flocks in migration.

**Voice:** Song loud, consisting of simple, slurred, burry whistles with pauses between notes tending to be longer than notes themselves. Calls include series of harsh, falling *shep* notes.

**Did you know?** Cassin's Vireo is the westernmost of three closely related species long classified as a single species, the Solitary Vireo. The other two are Plumbeous Vireo of the interior West and Blue-headed Vireo of the East.

## Date and Location Seen: _____

# HUTTON'S VIREO
## *Vireo huttoni*

**Description:** 12 cm. Small, compact, **greenish-grey** above, lighter below with **white wing-bars**. Prominent, **diffuse white eye-ring** broken above eye, extending forward to thick, stubby bill. **Feet bluish-grey**.

**Similar Species:** Ruby-crowned Kinglet (page 309) almost identical, smaller with thin bill, yellowish feet, black below lower wing-bar. Tends to flick wings more often. Male kinglet's red crown may be hidden. Cassin's Vireo (page 259) larger with longer bill, well-defined spectacled appearance.

**Seasonal Abundance:** Fairly common but often overlooked resident in region. Ranges from southwestern British Columbia down coast to California, also mountains from southeastern Arizona, southwestern Texas to Central America.

**Where to Find:** Lowlands to moderate elevations in foothills. Inconspicuous if not vocalizing. Typical sites include Point Grey, Campbell Valley, University of Victoria, Rathtrevor Beach Park, Miracle Beach Park.

**Habitat:** Mixed woodlands, forest edge, thickets.

**Diet and Behaviour:** Forages deliberately, mostly for insects, but takes some berries. Found often in pairs. Males sing constantly during brief period late winter–early spring. Joins mixed-species foraging flocks outside nesting season.

**Voice:** Song simple slurred, whistled *zweep,* repeated monotonously. Varied calls include rising *bree dee dee,* harsh mewing.

**Did you know?** Most vireos live in the tropics or migrate there for the winter. Hutton's is the only vireo to remain year round so far north.

**Date and Location Seen:** _____

261

**Description:** 13.5 cm. More compact than warblers. **Plain greyish-green above**, whitish below. **Prominent light eyebrow** only distinguishing mark. Sometimes erects crest in excitement. JUVENILE: Yellower below.

**Similar Species:** Red-eyed Vireo (page 265) larger with longer bill, grey cap, eyebrow bordered with black above, below. Other vireos have wing-bars. Warblers yellower, thinner-billed.

**Seasonal Abundance:** Common resident in region, May–September. Breeds from extreme southeastern Alaska to Maine, south in mountains to central Mexico; winters Mexico to northern Central America.

**Where to Find:** Widespread breeder from sea level to mountain passes except uncommon in urban areas. Common migrant throughout region.

**Habitat:** Breeds in mixed open woodland, forest edge, aspen groves. Also found in mostly coniferous woods, but utilizes available broadleaf trees for nesting.

**Diet and Behaviour:** Forages mostly in deciduous growth, primarily for insects; also some berries. Joins mixed flocks in migration. Sings often, even in migration, but difficult to spot due to slow foraging style.

**Voice:** Song extended, languid, rambling warble, different from other vireos—reminiscent of Purple Finch. Calls include nasal mewing.

**Did you know?** Vireos weave cup-shaped nests suspended from horizontal forked branches, sometimes placed at fairly low height.

**Date and Location Seen:** _____

**Description:** 14.5 cm. Compact, short-tailed. Large, flat-looking head with heavy black bill. **Plain greenish above** except for **grey cap**; whitish below. **White eyebrow bordered with black line above, another below** passing through red eye. Sometimes erects crest in excitement. JUVENILE: Brown eye.

**Similar Species:** Warbling Vireo (page 263) smaller with shorter bill, lacks grey cap, black lines bordering eyebrow. Other vireos have wing-bars; warblers smaller.

**Seasonal Abundance:** Fairly common resident in region, late May–August. North American population breeds across Canada, northwestern, eastern U.S., winters in Amazon Basin. Other races resident in South America.

**Where to Find:** Nests locally in lowlands, mostly in major river valleys; rare migrant away from breeding sites. Maplewood Flats, Ladner Harbour Park, Burnaby Lake, Duncan Sewage Lagoons good bets.

**Habitat:** Prefers mature broadleaf woods, especially cottonwoods along rivers. Also forests, parks with mature maple groves.

**Diet and Behaviour:** Forages mostly in canopy, primarily on insects, but also eats berries (especially in fall). Sings persistently, but difficult to spot due to slow foraging style.

**Voice:** Song continuous, short but complex; low, whistled phrases given every couple of seconds. Calls include mewed *nyeeah*.

**Did you know?** Male vireos share incubation duties with their mates and often sing while sitting on their nests.

**Date and Location Seen:** _____

**Description:** 30 cm. Medium-sized, **mostly blue**, long-tailed; upper body blackish with **long, prominent crest**, black banding on tail, wings. Sturdy blackish bill.

**Similar Species:** Blue Jay (not shown; rare winter visitor to region from east of Rockies) whitish below with broad white wing-bar, black necklace.

**Seasonal Abundance:** Fairly common resident in region but scarce breeder in cities, possibly impacted by crows. Ranges in West from Alaska to Nicaragua.

**Where to Find:** Throughout region to treeline. Some move southward or to lower elevations in winter.

**Habitat:** Coniferous, mixed forests, including urban, suburban neighbourhoods, parks, gardens with stands of large conifers.

**Diet and Behaviour:** Omnivorous; eats more seeds in fall, winter, frequents bird feeders. Garrulous, gregarious. Forages mostly in trees but also to ground. Becomes secretive around bulky stick nest during spring.

**Voice:** Noisy, often heard before seen, with wide repertoire of calls. Most common call harsh *shaark shaark shraak*, also rapid *wek wek wek wek wek*.

**Did you know?** Steller's Jay is the provincial bird of British Columbia. Although it is one of our most familiar birds, much remains to be learned about its habitat preferences and complex social system.

**Date and Location Seen:** _____

**Description:** 40 cm. Chunky, but shape can vary in flight. **Completely black** with stout bill, **short, square, fan-shaped tail**. JUVENILE: Brownish-black with red mouth lining.

**Similar Species:** American Crow (not shown; reaches eastern edge of region) extremely similar but slightly larger, voice less nasal. Common Raven (page 271) larger with wedge-shaped tail, longer bill, different voice; soars more, with wings held flat.

**Seasonal Abundance:** Common resident in region. Ranges coastally from Washington north to Alaska.

**Where to Find:** Abundant in cities, common along seashores, agricultural areas, but absent from dense, contiguous coniferous forest.

**Habitat:** Open woodlands, fields, clearings, cities, wherever trees available for nesting.

**Diet and Behaviour:** Omnivorous, eating anything available. Feeds on refuse, handouts, road kills, crops, fruit, seeds, insects. Intelligent, highly gregarious; forms huge night roosts after nesting season. Harasses predators noisily.

**Voice:** Raucous, garrulous. Common call *caww*.

**Did you know?** Crows in British Columbia are currently classified as two species, American Crow (interior) and Northwestern Crow (coastal). However, in the Puget Sound region of Washington these two forms interbreed freely and are nearly indistinguishable, leading many ornithologists to treat them as a single species.

**Date and Location Seen:** _____

**Description:** 61 cm. **Largest songbird**, with wingspan over 130 cm. **Entirely glossy black** with long wings, **long, wedge-shaped tail, long, heavy, formidable bill**. Puffy throat, head feathers erected in display impart even larger look.

**Similar Species:** Crows (page 269) much smaller with shorter bill, different voice; lack wedge-shaped tail. Ravens soar more often.

**Seasonal Abundance:** Fairly common resident in region. Ranges across northern hemisphere from Arctic to temperate zone, south in mountains to Central America.

**Where to Find:** Throughout region, scarcer around cities.

**Habitat:** Coniferous, mixed forests; coastal, agricultural areas.

**Diet and Behaviour:** Omnivorous, feeding on whatever available. Specializes in scavenging on large carcasses, descending on road kills, but also kills rodents, robs nests, feeds on insects. Highly intelligent, cautious; follows predators, hunters to take advantage of easy meal. Carries, hides food for future needs. Pairs, groups cavort in aerial displays.

**Voice:** Varied calls include harsh croak, liquid bell-like sounds, screamed *kraaah*, metallic rattles.

**Did you know?** Crows and ravens are always at odds. Ravens raid crow nests. Crows often swoop down on ravens while attempting to chase them away.

**Date and Location Seen:** _____

**Description:** 18.5 cm. **Brownish**, ground-dwelling songbird with **pink legs, slight crest** (sometimes flattened); strongly **streaked dark brown on breast**. White outer tail feathers, trailing edge of inner wing visible in flight.

**Similar Species:** Narrow bill, long wings, head shape separate Sky Lark from brownish-streaked sparrows. American Pipit (page 321) plainer above with darker legs, different call; bobs tail when walking. Horned Lark (page 389; seen in lowlands in migration) shows black breast band, moustache mark, forehead.

**Seasonal Abundance:** Fairly common but highly local year-round resident in region. Native to Eurasia. Celebrated for song, introduced in many places around world—usually unsuccessfully.

**Where to Find:** Restricted to Saanich Peninsula. Best areas Victoria Airport, Central Saanich Road bulb fields, Martindale Flats.

**Habitat:** Shortgrass fields, plowed agricultural fields.

**Diet and Behaviour:** Feeds on insects, other invertebrates, seeds, by walking on ground. Rarely perches in trees, bushes.

**Voice:** Loud, long, varied song, often delivered from high in air; low, chortling flight call.

**Did you know?** Sky Larks were introduced to Vancouver Island from Britain in 1903. Numbers expanded through the first half of the 1900s but have since contracted and have now stabilized at about 100 to 200 birds, although development still threatens some of the breeding sites. This is the only Sky Lark population in North America.

**Date and Location Seen:** _____

Male

Female

**Description:** 20 cm. **Large**, long-winged swallow with **shallowly forked tail**, relatively large bill. MALE: Adult **entirely dark purplish-blue**. First-year male resembles female with some blue below. FEMALE: **Grey of throat, chest extends around neck** in collar; belly dingy whitish; back, tail, face all-dark.

**Similar Species:** Larger than other swallows, soars more. European Starling (page 319) stubby with shorter tail. Black Swift (page 229) with longer, thinner, curving wings, more flickering wingbeat.

**Seasonal Abundance:** Fairly common but local resident in region mid-April to September. Ranges throughout eastern North America west to Prairie provinces, West Coast south from British Columbia; also locally in interior West. Winters in South America.

**Where to Find:** Scattered coastal locations, e.g., Maplewood Flats, Blackie Spit, Cowichan Bay, Nanaimo River estuary.

**Habitat:** Open areas, mostly near water.

**Diet and Behaviour:** Forages in flight for insects. Flocks in migration, sometimes with other swallows. Nests in small colonies, mostly in boxes, gourds provided by humans. Competes with other cavity nesters; sharply declined with European Starling introduction, but martins succeed in nest sites over water, often on pilings.

**Voice:** Song low-pitched, liquid warbles. Calls include rich, descending *cher cher*, rattle in alarm.

**Did you know?** Eastern Purple Martin populations are highly colonial, using multi-unit nest structures. Western populations are only loosely colonial, shunning multi-unit boxes.

**Date and Location Seen:** _____

Male

Female First-year

**Description:** 14.5 cm. Relatively stocky. Broad, triangular wings; short, slightly notched tail. **Glossy, iridescent blue above, bright white underparts**. FEMALE: Duller, with brown upperparts in first year changing to blue with age. JUVENILE: Plain brown above.

**Similar Species:** Violet-green Swallow (page 279) greener with white "saddlebag" flank patches, white cheek extending above eye. Juveniles difficult to separate. Northern Rough-winged Swallow (page 281) has dusky throat, upper breast.

**Seasonal Abundance:** Common summer resident in region, arrives by February, begins to depart by July, most gone before September. Rare in winter. Breeds from Alaska to Labrador, south through most of U.S.; winters southern U.S., West Indies, Mexico, Central America.

**Where to Find:** Widespread but local at mostly low or moderate elevation, usually near water.

**Habitat:** Open areas near water with trees, boxes for nest sites.

**Diet and Behaviour:** Forages in flight for insects. Eats some berries during migration, winter. Forms large flocks in migration, sometimes with other swallows. Nests in pairs but also in loose colonies, using natural cavities, nest boxes. Competes with other species for nest sites.

**Voice:** Song composed of series of chirps, warbles. Calls include liquid *chweet*, chattering in alarm.

**Did you know?** The Tree Swallow is the only songbird species in which one-year-old females have a different, distinct immature plumage.

**Date and Location Seen:** _____

Male

**Description:** 13.5 cm. Fairly **petite**, long-winged, with slightly notched tail. **White below**, including **saddlebag-like flank patches**. MALE: Glossy, iridescent purple-green above with **white extending above eye**. FEMALE: Duller; bronze-green with grey wash below, duskier cheek. JUVENILE: Lacks green.

**Similar Species:** Tree Swallow (page 277) bluer, with dark cheek, flanks.

**Seasonal Abundance:** Common summer resident in region, begins to return by late February, departs by October. Breeds in West from Alaska, Yukon to Mexico; winters Mexico, northern Central America.

**Where to Find:** Widespread, from coast up to fairly high elevations. Common breeder in cities.

**Habitat:** Open areas including woodlands, cities, agricultural lands; often near water in migration.

**Diet and Behaviour:** Forages in flight for insects, often at great height. Forms large flocks in migration, sometimes with other swallows. Nests in pairs but may be found in small colonies, nesting in cliff crevices, under building eaves, or in natural cavities, nest boxes. Scouts openings in buildings for potential nest sites.

**Voice:** Song repeated *tsip tseet tsip*, reminiscent of Pine Siskin. Calls include *chilip*—higher, sharper than Tree Swallow.

**Did you know?** Male Violet-green Swallows sing their courtship song monotonously in the pre-dawn darkness.

**Date and Location Seen:** _____

**Description:** 14.5 cm. Bulkier than most swallows, with smooth, deep wingbeats, square tail. **Plain brownish above**, whitish below, with **dingy grey throat, upper breast**. JUVENILE: Cinnamon on wings.

**Similar Species:** Cliff Swallow (page 283) has rusty-orange rump, white forehead spot. Female Purple Martin (page 275) larger, tail forked. Bank Swallow (not shown; rare in region) smaller with white throat, distinct brown breast band. Other white-bellied swallows have white throats.

**Seasonal Abundance:** Fairly common resident in region, April–August; a few linger to September. Breeds across North America from southern Alaska to Maritimes, south through Central America; northern populations move south in winter.

**Where to Find:** Throughout region, mostly at lower elevations.

**Habitat:** Open areas, usually near water, especially stream banks, road cuts.

**Diet and Behaviour:** Forages in flight low over water, fields for insects. Less likely to flock than other swallows, but joins mixed groups of swallows. Not colonial nester, but favourable site may attract more than one pair. Uses old burrow nests of other species, culvert pipe, other tubular man-made structures. Sometimes digs nest burrow.

**Voice:** Song rough, repeated *frrep*. Call harsh, low *breet*.

**Did you know?** The "rough-winged" moniker comes from the small serrations this species shows on its wing feathers.

**Date and Location Seen:** _____

# CLIFF SWALLOW
*Petrochelidon pyrrhonata*

**Description:** 14 cm. Compact swallow with **square, dark tail, rusty-buff rump. Dark chestnut throat, cheek** contrast with whitish underparts. **Light forehead spot**, buff collar stand out from dark cap, dark back streaked with white. Long, dark, pointed wings, tiny feet, bill.

**Similar Species:** Other swallows lack orange-buff rump.

**Seasonal Abundance:** Common resident in region, April–August; a few linger to September. Breeds across North America from Arctic to Mexico, winters in South America.

**Where to Find:** Widespread in open lowlands, ranging up some river drainages into mountains.

**Habitat:** Open areas, often near water; nests on cliffs or man-made structures, preferably of concrete, such as bridges, dams, buildings.

**Diet and Behaviour:** Forages in flight for insects. Flocks at all seasons, nests in colonies. Each pair builds gourd-shaped nest on vertical surface with some overhead protection, using mud pellets. Enters nest through short, narrow tunnel. Stages in large numbers away from nest sites when young fledge, then departs for South America.

**Voice:** Song thin, harsh twitters, given in series. Calls include husky *churr*, soft, low *veew* given in alarm.

**Did you know?** Other birds use Cliff Swallow nests for roosting in winter.


**Date and Location Seen:** _____

**Description:** 18 cm. **Streamlined**, graceful in flight. Blue-black above, **long, forked tail** with white spot near tip of each tail feather. Long, dark, pointed wings. **Cinnamon-buff below** with dark breast band, rusty throat, forehead, small black bill. Perches upright with tiny feet. JUVENILE: Pale beneath without tail streamers.

**Similar Species:** Purple Martin (page 275) larger, tail less forked. Other swallows lack forked tail.

**Seasonal Abundance:** Common resident in region, mid-April to mid-September; migrants continue through October. Rare in winter. Breeds around northern hemisphere from Arctic to subtropical zone; winters to southern hemisphere, mostly in tropics.

**Where to Find:** Throughout region; most common near man-made structures.

**Habitat:** Open habitats with buildings, bridges, culverts for nesting. Tends to be near water in migration.

**Diet and Behaviour:** Forages in flight for insects. Flocks in migration, often with other swallows. Builds nest from mud, grasses, lined with feathers, often inside or beneath structures such as bridges, farm buildings, eaves, porches, garages.

**Voice:** Song string of squeaky, twittering notes, grating sounds. Calls include *vit*, emphatic *pit veet* given in alarm.

**Did you know?** Barn Swallow populations in British Columbia have declined significantly for unknown reasons over the past 20 years.

**Date and Location Seen:** _____

**Description:** 13.5 cm. Typical chickadee, with **white cheek dividing dark cap from black bib**. Small, thin bill. **Cap black**, belly white, sides buffy, wings, tail, **back grey**. Coastal birds duskier than those in interior.

**Similar Species:** Chestnut-backed Chickadee (page 287) smaller with sooty-brown cap, chestnut sides, back. Mountain Chickadee (page 391) has white eyebrow.

**Seasonal Abundance:** Common resident in region. Ranges from Alaska to Newfoundland, south to New Mexico, Tennessee.

**Where to Find:** Common in Fraser Valley, absent from Vancouver Island, Gulf Islands, rare on mainland coast north of Greater Vancouver (recently colonizing Sunshine Coast).

**Habitat:** Broadleaf, mixed woods, thickets, neighbourhoods. Prefers deciduous growth, especially alders, cottonwoods.

**Diet and Behaviour:** Searches for insects, seeds among branches, hanging upside down to glean leaf undersides. Highly sociable when not nesting—forms small flocks, joins mixed flocks. Uses cavities, nest boxes, sometimes in backyards. Visits bird feeders, storing seeds in tree bark nearby.

**Voice:** Song clear, whistled *fee beee*, with second note lower. Calls include *chick a dee dee dee*.

**Did you know?** The *chick a dee* call is often used as an alarm call for the flock; the number of *dees* at the end increases in proportion to the seriousness of the danger.

**Date and Location Seen:** _____

**Description:** 12 cm. Typical chickadee with **white cheek dividing dark cap from black bib. Cap sooty-brown; sides, back rich chestnut**; small, thin bill, greyish wings, tail.

**Similar Species:** Black-capped Chickadee (page 273) slightly larger with black cap, lacks chestnut colour. Mountain Chickadee (page 379) with white eyebrow, lacks chestnut. Boreal Chickadee (page 391) has brownish-grey head, back, buffy sides.

**Seasonal Abundance:** Common resident in region. Ranges along coast from Alaska to central California, inland in moist forests to northwestern Montana.

**Where to Find:** Throughout region from just below treeline to coast, including cities.

**Habitat:** Coniferous forest; also mixed woods, but seldom far from conifers. Dispersing birds in fall may use deciduous woodlands.

**Diet and Behaviour:** Forages among branches for insects, seeds, some berries, hanging upside down while gleaning on twigs. Flocks with other small songbirds. Uses cavities, including nest boxes. Visits bird feeders.

**Voice:** *Chick zee zee* call higher, hoarser than other chickadees in region. Lacks whistled song of Black-capped.

**Did you know?** Chestnut-backed is the only chickadee on Vancouver Island and the Gulf Islands, occupying coniferous forest but also deciduous forest and garden habitats typical of Black-capped Chickadee on the Lower Mainland.

**Date and Location Seen:** _____

**Male**

**Female**

**Description:** 10 cm. **Tiny, plain greyish, nondescript** but lighter underneath, browner on head with **long tail**. Bill tiny, blackish, slightly downcurved. Eye white in female, dark in male, juvenile.

**Similar Species:** Chickadees have white cheek patches. Kinglets have wing-bars, shorter tails.

**Seasonal Abundance:** Common resident on southeastern Vancouver Island, Lower Mainland, at lower elevations. Ranges in West from southwestern British Columbia to Guatemala.

**Where to Find:** Lowlands; follows some river drainages into mountains. Numerous in urban areas. Generally absent from western, northern Vancouver Island, mainland coast north of Greater Vancouver.

**Habitat:** Broadleaf, mixed woodlands, open forest, parks, neighbourhoods.

**Diet and Behaviour:** Forages in flocks except during short period while nesting. Groups of up to 50 individuals move from tree to tree in tight line, almost in single file. Feeds mostly on insects but may eat seeds, berries. Visits suet feeders. Builds extraordinary hanging nest woven of moss, lichen, spider web, other materials, up to 30 centimetres long with small entrance near top, usually less than three metres from ground.

**Voice:** Calls given by flocking birds include short *tsip*, trilled alarm call.

**Did you know?** Bushtits are the smallest North American birds by weight except for the hummingbirds.

**Date and Location Seen:** _____

**Description:** 11 cm. **Stubby-tailed**, with straight, chisel-like bill. Grey above, **rusty underneath, white eyebrow** separates black cap from **black eye-line**. MALE: Brighter than female, juvenile.

**Similar Species:** Among other bark-clinging birds, Brown Creeper (page 295) streaked above, woodpeckers much larger. Chickadees have longer tails, white cheek patch.

**Seasonal Abundance:** Common resident in region. Numbers variably increase in lowland urban areas due to migration, downslope movement in winter. Breeds in coniferous forest zones across Canada, northern, western U.S. Winters south to Florida, Texas some years

**Where to Find:** Throughout region from treeline to coast, including urban areas.

**Habitat:** Coniferous, mixed forests, parks, woodlots.

**Diet and Behaviour:** Acrobatically climbs up, down tree trunks in search of insect prey, mostly in summer. More dependent on seeds in winter, particularly from conifers; may migrate from areas without adequate cone crop. Excavates nest cavity in rotten wood. Joins mixed-species flocks outside nesting season. Regular at sunflower, suet bird feeders.

**Voice:** Calls include short nasal *enk* given in series.

**Did you know?** Red-breasted Nuthatches smear conifer sap around their nest holes to deter predators.

**Date and Location Seen:** _____

**Description:** 13.5 cm. Slim, **streaked brownish-grey above** except for plain rusty rump, **white eyebrow**; white below, brightest on chin, breast. **Hitches up tree trunks** with long, stiff tail. Bill long, thin, downcurved.

**Similar Species:** Red-breasted Nuthatch (page 293) unstreaked, reddish below. Woodpeckers much larger. Bewick's Wren (page 297) sometimes goes up trees; has more uniform, brown upperparts, longer, freewheeling tail.

**Seasonal Abundance:** Fairly common resident throughout region. Some downslope movement occurs in winter. Breeds in forest zones from Alaska to Labrador, Middle Atlantic states, south through western U.S. to Central America. Some winter across rest of continent to northeastern Mexico.

**Where to Find:** Throughout region to mountain passes, including urban areas.

**Habitat:** Forests, open groves, parks containing good-sized trees.

**Diet and Behaviour:** Forages for insects while hitching up bark of tree using tail as brace. Probes crevices as it climbs, then flies down low onto next tree, begins again. Builds nest under sheets of loose bark on trunks, large branches. Joins mixed-species flocks outside nesting season.

**Voice:** Song high-pitched rising, falling notes in series, often ending on high note. Call high, thin *tseee*.

**Did you know?** The sight of the Brown Creeper's white breast as it moves up the tree may cause prey to move, facilitating detection.

**Date and Location Seen:** _____

**Description:** 13.5 cm. Slim, **plain brown**, with **bold white eyebrow**, long, thin downcurved bill, **long, brown tail** with fine dark bands above, **black-and-white edging, undersurface**. Often flicks tail from side to side.

**Similar Species:** House Wren (page 299), Marsh Wren (page 303) with much fainter eyebrows. Winter Wren (page 301) tiny, darker, with stubby tail.

**Seasonal Abundance:** Common resident on southeastern Vancouver Island, Lower Mainland. Ranges from southwestern British Columbia to California, across southwestern states to Texas, Mexico; spottily distributed east of Mississippi River.

**Where to Find:** Lowlands, including cities. Absent in western, northern Vancouver Island, mainland coast north of Greater Vancouver.

**Habitat:** Forest edge, open habitats, including hedgerows, thickets, backyards, other areas near human habitation.

**Diet and Behaviour:** Forages mostly for insects, some berries in dense undergrowth, but also probes bark on larger limbs, feeds on ground. Nests in thickets or cavities, often in man-made objects.

**Voice:** Song extremely variable, loud series of warbles, ringing trills, beginning with soft buzz that sounds like inhalation; easily confused with Song Sparrow. Calls numerous, including scolding, harsh notes, sharp *jik*.

**Did you know?** Bewick's Wren was once more common and widespread in eastern North America than in the West. For unknown reasons the situation has reversed in recent decades.

**Date and Location Seen:** _____

**Description:** 12 cm. Nondescript **plain brown, paler below**, with **thin bill**. Fine, dark banding on wings, tail, vague line through eye. **Light eye-ring**. Often holds tail at upward angle.

**Similar Species:** Bewick's Wren (page 297) larger, with bold white eyebrow. Winter Wren (page 301) darker, with short tail. Marsh Wren (page 303) in wet habitat, with whitish eyebrow, streaks on back; plain juveniles difficult to separate.

**Seasonal Abundance:** Fairly common but highly local summer resident in region. Northern populations breed across southern Canada, most of U.S., winter southern U.S., Mexico. Other forms resident Mexico to South America, often considered separate species.

**Where to Find:** Southeastern Vancouver Island, Gulf Islands; essentially absent from mainland coast.

**Habitat:** Drier forest edge, semi-open habitats at lower elevations including clear-cuts, areas near human habitation.

**Diet and Behaviour:** Forages on ground, bushes for insects. Nests in cavities, including nest boxes. Competes for nest sites with other species. Males vigorously protect territory with constant singing.

**Voice:** Song exuberant, bubbling trills, whistled notes, given in rapid series. Calls include scolding, rattling, nasal mewing.

**Did you know?** The male House Wren fills many prospective nest holes with materials and the female lays eggs in one.

**Date and Location Seen:** _____

**Description:** 10 cm. **Tiny**, round, with **stubby tail**, thin bill, light brown eyebrow. Chocolate-brown above, fine, dark banding on tail, wings, belly. Breast **rich rufous-brown**. Secretive but constantly active.

**Similar Species:** Bewick's Wren (page 297) larger, with bold white eyebrow. House Wren (page 299) with light breast. Marsh Wren (page 303) with whitish eyebrow, streaked back.

**Seasonal Abundance:** Common resident in region; lowland numbers increase in winter. Breeds in coniferous forest zones of Alaska, Canada, northern U.S., south in mountains, along West Coast; winters milder parts of breeding range, midwestern, southeastern, southwestern U.S. Also resident in Eurasia.

**Where to Find:** Throughout region. Breeds to treeline, withdraws to below level of heavy snow in winter. Frequent then in neighbourhoods, parks.

**Habitat:** Nests in wet underbrush of coniferous forest. Dense forest, thickets, tangles in winter, migration.

**Diet and Behaviour:** Moves mouse-like through low undergrowth, eating insects; may also eat berries. Investigates intruders from open perch while bobbing up-and-down. Males sing from low, hidden or mid-level, exposed perches.

**Voice:** Song remarkable lengthy series of varied tinkling trills, warbles. Calls include oft-given *chit chit*, rapid, staccato series of chips.

**Did you know?** Curiosity sometimes brings Winter Wrens inside buildings, where they can become trapped.

**Date and Location Seen:** _____

*Cistothorus palustris*

**Description:** 12 cm. **Secretive** but curious. Brown above with **fine dark banding on wings, tail**, plain greyish below; **tail held cocked up**. Dark cap, white eyebrow, faint white streaks on upper back. Long, thin bill curves down. JUVENILE: Appears almost plain brown with vague light eyebrow.

**Similar Species:** House Wren (page 299) plainer with only very faint eyebrow. Bewick's Wren (page 297) larger, with bolder white eyebrow. Winter Wren (page 301) darker, with short tail.

**Seasonal Abundance:** Common resident in region. Breeds across continent from British Columbia to New England, south to California, Gulf Coast (but absent in interior southeastern U.S.); winters south to Mexico.

**Where to Find:** In appropriate habitat throughout southeastern Vancouver Island, Lower Mainland.

**Habitat:** Open freshwater or brackish marshes with thick emergent vegetation, usually cattails. Also salt marshes, river edge, wet fields, scrub adjacent to wetlands.

**Diet and Behaviour:** Forages low, crawling within thick cover, mostly for insects. Male sings day or night from exposed or hidden perches with tail cocked, often flat against back.

**Voice:** Song mechanical—but musical—rattled trill begun with a few call notes. Call distinctive *tik*.

**Did you know?** The male Marsh Wren builds multiple spherical nests amidst emergent stalks; the female chooses one to line and lay eggs in.

**Date and Location Seen:** _____

**Description:** 19 cm. Stout, **chunky, uniform slate-grey, with short tail**, thin, straight bill, pale legs. Shape, **bobbing motions** suggest large wren. Often flashes white eyelids. JUVENILE: Spotted breast.

**Similar Species:** Distinctive; larger than any wren in region.

**Seasonal Abundance:** Uncommon resident in region, mostly mountains, foothills in summer; may be seen in more urbanized areas in winter. Ranges in western mountains from Aleutians to Central America.

**Where to Find:** During nesting season, rushing streams (less frequently ponds) from middle elevations up to treeline. Moves downstream in winter to larger rivers (especially those with salmon runs), suburban creeks. Good bets then Chilliwack, Chehalis, Capilano, Squamish, Cheakamus, Goldstream, Campbell rivers.

**Habitat:** Rushing streams, rivers, pond margins. Occasional at stream mouths in winter.

**Diet and Behaviour:** Swims or walks on stream bottoms in pursuit of aquatic insect larvae, molluscs, small fish, fish eggs. Stands, bobs on streamside rocks, flying up, down stream to feed, protect territory. Builds bulky, domed nests next to streams, often under bridges. Uses wings to "fly" underwater.

**Voice:** Song loud, piercing musical whistles repeated in series. Calls include buzzy *bzzeet*.

**Did you know?** Dippers are the only truly aquatic songbirds.

**Date and Location Seen:** _____

**Description:** 9.5 cm. Tiny, with **short, notched tail**, thin bill, constant, **nervous wing flitting**. Olive-grey above, greyish-white below, **white wing-bars**, dark flight feathers with golden edging. Broad **white eyebrow below black-striped crown**. Crown center orange-and-yellow in male, yellow in female; colours may be obscured.

**Similar Species:** Ruby-crowned Kinglet (page 309) slightly larger, greener; has eye-ring, no head stripes. Warblers larger.

**Seasonal Abundance:** Common resident in region. Breeds in coniferous forest zones from southeastern Alaska across continent to Newfoundland, south in mountains to Guatemala; winters through all but northernmost parts of breeding range south across U.S. to northeastern Mexico.

**Where to Find:** Throughout region: lowlands, mountains, cities.

**Habitat:** Breeds in conifer stands, winters in coniferous, mixed woods; migrants appear anywhere.

**Diet and Behaviour:** Forages high, low, although when nesting tends to remain high. Gregarious when not nesting. Prefers conifers but seeks out insects in low deciduous growth, climbing, gleaning, hanging upside down, moving rapidly in flocks. Joins mixed flocks.

**Voice:** Song begins with three high, thin notes, ends with tumbling chatter. Call thin *tsee tsee tsee* or *tsee*.

**Did you know?** The English and Latin names of kinglets reflect the jewelled crowns and assertive behaviour of these "little kings."

**Date and Location Seen:** _____

**Description:** 10 cm. **Tiny**, plump-appearing, with **short tail**, thin bill, constant, **nervous wing flitting**. Greenish-grey above, lighter below. Dark wings with white wing-bars, blackish below lower bar. Prominent but diffuse white eye-ring. Red crown of male usually obscured.

**Similar Species:** Golden-crowned Kinglet (page 307) has light eyebrow below black stripe, no eye-ring. Hutton's Vireo (page 261) very similar but larger with thicker bill, blue-grey not yellowish feet; lacks black below wing-bar.

**Seasonal Abundance:** Common migrant, winter resident in lowlands of region, September to mid-May. Nests high in mountains. Breeding range from Alaska, British Columbia to Labrador, south in mountains of West; winters Pacific Coast, southern U.S., to Guatemala.

**Where to Find:** Winters throughout lowlands in urban, agricultural settings, remote areas. Widespread in migration; breeds in mountains, particularly on mainland.

**Habitat:** Breeds in coniferous forest; prefers thickets, brush, forest edge in winter.

**Diet and Behaviour:** Forages low or high, mostly for insects. Eats some berries. Congregates in attractive habitats. Joins mixed-species flocks.

**Voice:** Song long, rolling series of trills, twitters, repeated phrases, often heard in spring migration. Call low, husky *jidit*.

**Did you know?** Curious and easily attracted, male Ruby-crowned Kinglets display their red crowns aggressively when agitated.

**Date and Location Seen:** _____

**Description:** 17 cm. **Plain warm brown above** from head to tail. Buff breast with small dark spots. Thin bill, brown face with diffuse, **buffy eye-ring** extending to bill, giving **spectacled appearance**.

**Similar Species:** Hermit Thrush (page 313) with contrasting rusty tail, thin white eye-ring, whiter breast, habit of cocking tail. Juvenile American Robin (page 315) much larger, some orange on breast.

**Seasonal Abundance:** Common summer resident throughout region to mountain passes. Breeds from Alaska across Canada, northern U.S. to Newfoundland, south to California in West. Winters from Mexico to South America.

**Where to Find:** Throughout region, mid-May to early September; a few linger later. Mostly breeds away from urbanized areas. Migrants secretive but widespread.

**Habitat:** Forested habitats of all types up to mid-mountain altitude. Prefers dense understory cover with salmonberry, other native shrubs.

**Diet and Behaviour:** Forages on ground but also often in trees, unlike Hermit Thrush. Feeds on insects, berries. Migrates at night. Shy; more often heard than seen.

**Voice:** Song distinctive series of nasal whistles spiralling upward. Calls include low, whistled *bic*, nasal *why*.

**Did you know?** Stories from coastal indigenous people say that the song of the Swainson's Thrush ripens the salmonberries.

**Date and Location Seen:** _____

**Description:** 17 cm. **Plain greyish-brown upperparts contrast with reddish-brown rump, tail**. Buffy-white breast with dark spots, grey flanks. Thin bill, **thin white eye-ring** on brownish face. Head greyish or brownish dependent on race.

**Similar Species:** Swainson's Thrush (page 311) lacks reddish tail; rarely cocks tail. Coastal populations browner. Fox Sparrow (page 349) has conical bill.

**Seasonal Abundance:** Common breeder at higher elevations in region. Common but secretive migrant, rare winter resident in lowlands. Breeds across continent from Alaska to Newfoundland; winters coasts, southern U.S., south to Central America.

**Where to Find:** Breeds in mountains, winters in lowlands; migrants widespread.

**Habitat:** Coniferous, mixed forests, including older, regenerating clear-cuts. In winter, thickets, forest edge, parks, neighbourhoods.

**Diet and Behaviour:** Forages on or near ground for insects, fruit. Cocks, then slowly lowers tail while pumping wings, giving call note (unlike Swainson's Thrush). Seldom flocks, but may feed in fruiting shrubs with other species. Migrates at night.

**Voice:** Song consists of high, clear whistle followed by ethereal, spiralling whistles given at different pitches. Calls include rising *zhweeee*, muffled *chup*.

**Did you know?** Hermit Thrushes sometimes stir leaf litter with one foot to flush prey.

**Date and Location Seen:** _____

Male

Juvenile

**Description:** 25 cm. Bulky thrush, with solid grey back. **Upright stance**. Thin but fairly stout yellow bill, dark stripes on white throat, **dull orange breast**, white undertail, **white marks above, below eye**. MALE: Darker, head blackish. FEMALE: Breast lighter orange. JUVENILE: Spotted breast.

**Similar Species:** Other thrushes smaller, without orange breast. Spotted Towhee (page 343) smaller with white belly.

**Seasonal Abundance:** Common resident in region. Breeds across North America, south in mountains of Mexico; winters from southern part of breeding range south to Guatemala.

**Where to Find:** Ubiquitous. Backyards to mountains.

**Habitat:** Forests, cities, lawns, open areas. Nests wherever trees, structures present for nest placement, mud available for construction.

**Diet and Behaviour:** Runs on ground or stands still while searching for insects, worms. Takes fruits from bushes, trees, ground. Winter flocks can number in thousands. Roosts communally at night in dense vegetation, often near fruit. May migrate if driven south by cold, but usually returns north as soon as temperature allows.

**Voice:** Song familiar lengthy, rich carolling, consisting of rising, falling phrases. Calls include *tuk tuk tuk*, sharp *piik* given in alarm, high, thin *sreep* in flight.

**Did you know?** The American Robin takes its name from an Old World species that is also orange-breasted, though not closely related.

**Date and Location Seen:** _____

**Male**

**Female**

**Description:** 24 cm. **Chunky, with short tail, dark breast band, dark mask**, bill. **Orange eyebrow**, breast, throat, wing patches, broad wing-bars. MALE: **Bluish-grey**, cap to tail; breast band, mask black. FEMALE: Brownish-grey mask, upperparts, with faint breast band.

**Similar Species:** American Robin (page 315) with longer tail, no breast band.

**Seasonal Abundance:** Common resident in region, breeding in extensive coniferous forest; more widespread in suburban, rural habitats in winter. Breeding range extends from Alaska, Yukon to northern California; vacates high mountains, northern parts of range in winter as birds move downslope or farther south (as far as southern California).

**Where to Find:** Throughout region in summer, below level of heavy snow in winter, including neighbourhoods, parks.

**Habitat:** Moist coniferous forest with thick understory.

**Diet and Behaviour:** Forages for insects, fruits in trees, on ground. Eats mostly fruit in winter, sometimes visits sunflower feeders; may congregate near arbutus, ornamentals. Flocks less than robins, but gregarious at times in migration, winter. Male sings year round from high perches.

**Voice:** Song fairly long, ethereal, trilled whistle, repeated at different pitches after long pauses. Calls include *chup* similar to Hermit Thrush.

**Did you know?** Varied Thrushes wander regularly as far as the East Coast.

**Date and Location Seen:** _____

Breeding

Non-breeding

Juvenile

**Description:** 20 cm. Chunky, with **short tail, long, thin, pointed bill**. Short tail, gliding habit impart **triangular appearance in flight**. BREEDING: Plain **iridescent blackish** with minimal brown feather edging, **yellow bill**. NON-BREEDING: Heavy white spotting, prominent brown feather edging throughout; dark bill. JUVENILE: **Plain greyish-brown**, dark bill.

**Similar Species:** Western Meadowlark (page 365) with white outer tail feathers, yellow breast. Blackbirds with longer tails, more conical bills.

**Seasonal Abundance:** Common year-round resident in region. Original range Eurasia; introduced in many other parts of world including North America, where now found from Alaska, Labrador to West Indies, Mexico.

**Where to Find:** Throughout region. Abundant in urban, agricultural areas, scarce in mountains, dense forest.

**Habitat:** Disturbed habitats including cities, parks, open woods, farms.

**Diet and Behaviour:** Probes ground for insects. Forages in trees, on ground for whatever food available, often fly-catches like swallows. Highly gregarious, gathering in noisy flocks of thousands, especially at evening roosts. Often nests twice per year, competing for nest cavities with native species.

**Voice:** Sings year round—continuous series of squeaks, squawks, including mimicry of other species.

**Did you know?** Introduced in New York City in 1890, European Starlings expanded across the continent, reaching coastal British Columbia in the 1950s.

**Date and Location Seen:** _____

**Description:** 16.5 cm. **Slender**, sparrow-like, with **long, dark, white-edged tail**, long, thin bill. Plain grey-brown above with faint wing-bars, variably **streaked below**, mostly on buff-white upper breast. Light eyebrow, eye-ring, moustache mark. **Bobs tail while walking**.

**Similar Species:** Thin bill, tail-bobbing habit separate pipits from sparrows. Sky Lark (page 273) with back more heavily streaked, crested appearance.

**Seasonal Abundance:** Fairly common spring, fall migrant in region. Breeds in mountains above treeline. Uncommon to rare in winter in lowlands. Breeds across North America to eastern Siberia, south in mountains to New Mexico. Winters both coasts, southern interior U.S., Mexico.

**Where to Find:** In summer on alpine tundra, e.g., Manning Park, Garibaldi Park. Widespread in migration away from urban areas. In winter on farm fields on Fraser Delta, southern Vancouver Island.

**Habitat:** Breeds in high-altitude tundra; migrants, winter birds use plowed fields, meadows, dried pond margins, beaches.

**Diet and Behaviour:** Usually walks on ground, foraging for seeds, insects. Flocks at all seasons except when nesting. Can be tame, approachable, but entire flock may flush if alarm call given.

**Voice:** Sharp distinctive *pi pit* call, given often in flight.

**Did you know?** American Pipits in breeding plumage are somewhat more lightly streaked beneath than in non-breeding plumage. Some breeding individuals may be completely unstreaked.

**Date and Location Seen:** _____

Bohemian Waxwing

Juvenile

**Description:** 18.5 cm. **Sleek, crested**. Silky brown head, back grade into grey rump. Black mask, chin, **yellow belly, white undertail**. Plain grey wings with **waxy red spots**. Blackish, square, **short tail with yellow tip**. JUVENILE: Duller with streaks below.

**Similar Species:** Distinctive. **Bohemian Waxwing** (see inset; rare winter visitor in region) larger, **greyer**, with **chestnut undertail**. European Starling (page 319) has same triangular, short-tailed shape in flight, but larger with different markings.

**Seasonal Abundance:** Common summer resident in region, becomes rare most winters. Returns in mid-May, almost all have moved south by November. Largest flocks appear in fall, include many juveniles. Breeds across southern Canada, northern U.S., winters south to West Indies, Panama.

**Where to Find:** Throughout region, including urban areas.

**Habitat:** Open forest, forest edge, forested shorelines; city parks, neighbourhoods near ornamental plantings.

**Diet and Behaviour:** Eats mostly berries, other small fruits, but often fly-catches during summer—especially from trees along shores of ponds, small lakes. Tends to flock except when nesting, descends on ripe fruit en masse. Nests late to exploit the availability of ripe fruit. Tight, swirling flocks can number in hundreds. Calls frequently in flight, while perched.

**Voice:** Call high-pitched, thin *sreeee*.

**Did you know?** Adult Cedar Waxwing males can be distinguished from females by their glossy black throat.

**Date and Location Seen:** _____

Breeding form

Grey-headed form

**Description:** 12 cm. **Plain** with obscure markings, faint, blurred breast streaks, no wing-bars, **small, pointed bill**. Best mark **vague dark line through eye**; male's dull orange crown sometimes visible. Breeding form in region **evenly yellow except for olive back**. Migratory northern form grey-headed, duller, **brightest yellow under tail**.

**Similar Species:** Yellow Warbler (page 327) very plain-faced with larger bill. Female Wilson's Warbler (page 339) shows vague dark cap, often flits tail. MacGillivray's Warbler (page 335) with more distinct hood. Warbling Vireo (page 263) grey with heavier bill.

**Seasonal Abundance:** Common summer resident in region, rare in winter. Migrants return by late March; fall migration protracted, can continue into November. Breeds across Canada, south in western U.S. to Mexican border; winters Pacific Coast, southeastern U.S., Mexico south to El Salvador.

**Where to Find:** Breeds throughout region, away from cities, to treeline. Migrants can be anywhere. In winter, dense, overgrown thickets, hedgerows.

**Habitat:** Brushy forest edge including regenerating clear-cuts. Blackberry thickets preferred in winter.

**Diet and Behaviour:** Forages relatively low on insects, some fruit. Also feeds on nectar. Joins mixed-species flocks in migration.

**Voice:** Song colourless trill that drops off at end. Call high, sharp chip.

**Did you know?** Orange-crowned Warblers sometimes feed at sapsucker wells in winter.

**Date and Location Seen:** _____

Male

Female

# YELLOW WARBLER
### *Dendroica petechia*

**Description:** 12 cm. Short-tailed, **all-yellow**, darker above; wings with lighter feather edges. **Dark eye prominent on plain face**. Yellow tail spots. MALE: Bright yellow with distinct **reddish-brown breast streak**s. FEMALE: Duller, no breast streaks; can show **indistinct yellow eye-ring**.

**Similar Species:** Wilson's Warbler (page 339) female with longer tail, faint dark cap. Orange-crowned Warbler (page 325) with dark line through eye. Common Yellowthroat (page 337) female with grey-white belly.

**Seasonal Abundance:** Common resident in region, May–September. Spring migrants continue to pass through into June; fall movement begins in July. Breeds across North America except Gulf Coast, Mojave Desert, south to South America. North American breeders winter from southern California, Mexico, West Indies to Amazonian Brazil.

**Where to Find:** Breeds throughout region in appropriate habitat. Migrants more widespread.

**Habitat:** Cottonwood stands, shrubby areas near water.

**Diet and Behaviour:** Forages at various heights, primarily for insects, some fruit. Males feed higher in canopy than females. Joins mixed flocks in migration.

**Voice:** Song *sweet sweet sweet I'm so sweet*. Call notes include thin *tsip*, loud chip.

**Did you know?** Brown-headed Cowbirds often lay eggs in Yellow Warbler nests. To foil them, the warblers sometimes build a new nest over the top of all the eggs and lay a fresh set.

## Date and Location Seen: _____

Audubon's
Male Breeding

Non-breeding

Myrtle
Male Breeding

**Description:** 13.5 cm. **Yellow on rump**, sides of breast; **white tail spots. Brown in winter with streaked breast**. Male in breeding plumage has small yellow crown patch (sometimes obscured), grey back, **black breast with sides streaked down to white belly**. Two distinct forms in region. MYRTLE WARBLER: **White throat**, white wing-bars, **black mask**; female browner than male, lacks bib. AUDUBON'S WARBLER: **Yellow throat**, grey head, **solid white wing patch**; female browner than male with streaked breast, less yellow on throat. In winter, head plainer than Myrtle.

**Similar Species:** Distinctive in breeding plumage. In winter, separable from sparrows by thin bill, yellow rump.

**Seasonal Abundance:** AUDUBON'S common summer resident in region; both forms common in migration, uncommon in winter. Breeds North America to Central America (MYRTLE in north, AUDUBON'S in West), winters south to West Indies, Panama.

**Where to Find:** Throughout region.

**Habitat:** Breeds locally in coniferous forest, winters in agricultural areas, brushy woods, coastal scrub.

**Diet and Behaviour:** Forages for insects, berries among leaves, twigs; also fly-catches. Fruit intake increases in winter (wax myrtle preferred). Flocks outside breeding season.

**Voice:** Variable, two-part song—clear, warbled trill, usually rising or falling at end. MYRTLE chip note loud *tup*, AUDUBON'S weaker *chwit*.

**Did you know?** The two forms have often been considered separate species.

**Date and Location Seen:** _____

Male

Female Immature

# BLACK-THROATED GRAY WARBLER
## *Dendroica nigrescens*

**Description:** 12 cm. **Black-and-white head pattern** with **small yellow spot in front of eye**; grey back, white wing-bars, **white underneath with dark side streaks**; white underside of tail. MALE: Black cap, cheek, extensive bib. FEMALE: Crown, cheek greyer, throat white with bib reduced (can be absent in immature).

**Similar Species:** Townsend's Warbler (page 333) with yellow underparts.

**Seasonal Abundance:** Fairly common resident in region, mid-April to September; a few linger later. Breeds southwestern British Columbia, Colorado south to northwestern Mexico, winters southern California, Texas south through central Mexico.

**Where to Find:** Throughout region at lower elevations, except absent on western Vancouver Island.

**Habitat:** Breeds in mature deciduous, mixed forest. Migrants use more varied habitats.

**Diet and Behaviour:** Forages for insects at various heights in canopy. Gleans, hovers, sallies for prey. Joins mixed-species flocks in migration.

**Voice:** Song variable, husky series of buzz notes with emphatic ending. Calls include low, dull chip.

**Did you know?** In the southern portion of their breeding range Black-throated Gray Warblers are associated with oak forests—quite different from their haunts of alder and maple woods with scattered conifers in the Pacific Northwest.

## Date and Location Seen: _____

Male

Female

**Description:** 12 cm. **Black-and-yellow head pattern, yellow breast with dark streaks at sides**, greenish back, white wing-bars, whitish belly. MALE: Black cap, cheek, bib, divided by bright yellow. FEMALE: Crown, cheek lighter, bib reduced (absent in immature).

**Similar Species:** Black-throated Gray Warbler (page 331) lacks yellow except for dot in front of eye.

**Seasonal Abundance:** Common summer resident in region, rare in winter. Breeds Alaska to Idaho, winters down coast to Mexico, Central America, mostly south of Canada–U.S. border.

**Where to Find:** Throughout region, but rarely nesting near urban areas; easier to find in intact coniferous forests, although migrants widespread.

**Habitat:** Mature coniferous forest. Wintering birds often associate with cedars. In breeding season frequents high canopy where difficult to see, but song betrays its presence.

**Diet and Behaviour:** Gleans, hover-gleans for insects high in canopy. Joins mixed-species flocks in migration, winter.

**Voice:** Buzzy song variable with several evenly pitched notes followed by thin, high notes. Call quiet but sharp chip.

**Did you know?** Townsend's Warbler songs are highly variable. Some versions are very similar to those of the Black-throated Gray Warbler.

**Date and Location Seen:** _____

Male

**Description:** 12.5 cm. Skulking warbler, **olive above** with **plain wings, grey hood, white crescents above, below eye, yellow lower breast, belly**. MALE: Hood bluish-grey. Blackish marks through eye, on bib. FEMALE: Duller with less distinct eye crescents.

**Similar Species:** Grey-headed form of Orange-crowned Warbler (page 325) similar with less distinct hood, eye crescents. Nashville Warbler (not shown; rare in region) lacks hood, has yellow throat, complete white eye-ring.

**Seasonal Abundance:** Fairly common in region, mid-April to early September. Breeds in western North America from southeastern Alaska to southwestern U.S., winters Mexico to Panama.

**Where to Find:** Locally from lowlands to near treeline. Migrants secretive.

**Habitat:** Forest edge with dense understory, including recent clear-cuts, burns, brushy Scotch-broom-dominated fields.

**Diet and Behaviour:** Forages under cover in dense, low growth for insects. Male sometimes sings from exposed elevated perch. Pairs greet intruders with loud call notes.

**Voice:** Song rhythmic series of buzzy trills with last notes lower-pitched, slurred. Calls include loud, sharp *tsik*.

**Did you know?** MacGillivray's Warbler is named for the Scottish ornithologist William MacGillivray. Its scientific name memorializes William Fraser Tolmie, a prominent pioneer, politician, and naturalist in the early days of Victoria, British Columbia.

**Date and Location Seen:** _____

**Male**

**Female**

# COMMON YELLOWTHROAT
### *Geothlypis trichas*

**Description:** 12 cm. Wren like warbler, olive above with **plain wings, whitish-grey belly, yellow throat, breast, undertail**. MALE: **Black "bandit" mask** bordered by white above. FEMALE: Without mask, browner.

**Similar Species:** Other yellowish warblers lack mask, whitish-grey belly.

**Seasonal Abundance:** Common resident in region, April–September; rarely lingers into winter. Breeds across Canada, lower 48 states, winters south to West Indies, Panama.

**Where to Find:** Locally throughout region. Iona Island, Reifel Sanctuary, Swan Lake, Buttertubs Marsh typical sites. Rare in migration away from nesting habitat.

**Habitat:** Low, dense, wetland vegetation, but also uses brushy, Scotch-broom-dominated fields.

**Diet and Behaviour:** Creeps through thick cover foraging for insects. Sometimes feeds on ground. Male sings from elevated perches.

**Voice:** Song whistled *witchety witchety witchety witchety*. Calls include often-given *cheep*, electric-like *bizz*.

**Did you know?** In courtship, male Common Yellowthroats perform a flight display in which they rise up to 30 metres in the air, calling and singing.

**Date and Location Seen:** _____

Male

**Description:** 12 cm. **Yellow below**, brightest on plain face, **olive-green above, wings plain**. Frequently flits wings, tail. MALE: **Round inky-black cap**. FEMALE: **Indistinct cap** makes yellow eyebrow stand out. IMMATURE: Lighter cap.

**Similar Species:** Yellow Warbler (page 327) female with shorter tail, lacks any trace of cap. Orange-crowned Warbler (page 325) with dark line through eye, thinner bill.

**Seasonal Abundance:** Common resident in region, mid-April to mid-September. Extremely rare in winter. Breeds across northern North America, south in western mountains to northern New Mexico, central California. Winters Gulf Coast, Mexico south to Panama.

**Where to Find:** Throughout region, but nesting uncommon in urban areas. Common migrant in all habitats.

**Habitat:** Forests of all ages with dense undergrowth.

**Diet and Behaviour:** Flits through foliage at various heights feeding mostly on insects. Sallies, gleans from small branches. Eats some berries. Sings constantly in spring.

**Voice:** Song emphatic series of slurred chips that builds in volume, speed. Call nasal *timp*, quite different from other warblers.

**Did you know?** Wilson's Warbler and four other North American bird species are named for pioneering ornithologist Alexander Wilson.

**Date and Location Seen:** _____

Male Breeding

Female

**Description:** 17 cm. Compact, with **fairly stout bill**. MALE: Black back, tail, wings, **yellow, white wing-bars**. Adult **bright yellow with scarlet head** in breeding plumage; immature, non-breeding-plumaged birds lack red on head. FEMALE: Lacks red head. Olive replaces black areas of male; back, belly can be grey. Wing-bars reduced but still conspicuous.

**Similar Species:** Bullock's Oriole (page 371) has much more pointed bill, orange tail. Warblers smaller.

**Seasonal Abundance:** Common resident in region, May–early September; uncommon into October. Breeds in West from northwestern Canada to Mexican border, winters Mexico to Costa Rica.

**Where to Find:** Throughout region, but rarely nests successfully in urban areas. Easiest to spot at forest edges. Migrants can be inconspicuous in canopy.

**Habitat:** Fairly open coniferous or mixed forest; migrants use varied habitats.

**Diet and Behaviour:** Gleans methodically in treetops, mostly for insects; occasionally sallies. Also takes fruit, especially in fall. Migrants often move in small flocks.

**Voice:** Song short series of slow phrases similar to that of American Robin, but hoarser. Call distinctive *pid er ick*.

**Did you know?** Tanagers are a New World group of over 200 species, most of which live in the tropics. Western Tanager is the northernmost of the four tanager species that occur regularly north of Mexico.

**Date and Location Seen:** _____

Male

Juvenile

**Description:** 20 cm. **Dark hood**, upper body contrast with **rufous sides, white belly. Bold white spots on back, white outer corners on black tail**. Dark conical bill, red eye. Male black, female greyer. JUVENILE: Heavily streaked, lacks hood.

**Similar Species:** Dark-eyed Junco (page 359) smaller, bill pinkish, entire tail edge white, lacks white back spots. Smaller size, lack of white tail corners separate streaked sparrows from juvenile towhee.

**Seasonal Abundance:** Common resident in region except at higher elevations in winter. Ranges from southern British Columbia throughout western North America to Guatemala; northern interior birds move south in winter.

**Where to Find:** Throughout region, primarily lowlands; absent from closed-canopy forests. Thrives in urban areas, nesting in backyards.

**Habitat:** Open woods with dense, shrubby understory; thickets, overgrown fields.

**Diet and Behaviour:** Forages mostly on ground for seeds, insects, fruits. Has been recorded taking lizards, other small vertebrates. Scratches ground vigorously with both feet while feeding. Does not flock, although found with other sparrows. Eats spilled grain on ground below bird feeders.

**Voice:** Song variable, buzzy trill. Call, given often, rising *schreeee*.

**Did you know?** The Spotted Towhee is quite variable throughout its large range. It and the closely related Eastern Towhee were long treated as a single species, the Rufous-sided Towhee.

**Date and Location Seen:** _____

American Tree Sparrow

**Breeding**

**Juvenile**

**Description:** 13.5 cm. **Slim**, fairly long-tailed sparrow with streaked back, **unstreaked grey breast**. BREEDING: **Rufous cap bordered by white eyebrow**, black line through eye. NON-BREEDING: Browner; cap dull, streaked. JUVENILE: Resembles non-breeding but with streaked breast, pinkish bill.

**Similar Species:** **American Tree Sparrow** (see inset; rare winter resident in region) similar but with **central breast spot**, less distinct rufous eye-line. Other small sparrows in region shorter-tailed, less slim-appearing.

**Seasonal Abundance:** Uncommon, local summer resident in region, mainly on southern Vancouver Island, Gulf Islands. Breeds across continent from central Alaska, Newfoundland, south through U.S., in mountains to Nicaragua. Winters southern U.S., Mexico southward through breeding range.

**Where to Find:** Mostly drier places, including southeastern Vancouver Island, Manning Park. Rare migrant in Greater Vancouver, no longer breeds.

**Habitat:** Open woods, woodland edge with grassy areas.

**Diet and Behaviour:** Forages mostly on ground for seeds, insects. Sometimes sallies for flying insects.

**Voice:** Song mechanical-sounding long trill, all on one pitch. Calls include sharp chip, thin *seet*.

**Did you know?** Chipping Sparrows make use of animal hair in building their nests. Woven hair makes up the bulk of the nest in some cases.

**Date and Location Seen:** _____

**Description:** 13.5 cm. **Small, streaked below**, above. **Short notched tail**, whitish central crown stripe, **yellowish eyebrow**, pinkish bill, legs. Eyebrow yellower in spring, summer.

**Similar Species:** Song Sparrow (page 351) larger; richer brown with dense, thick streaks on breast. Lincoln's Sparrow (page 353) grey-headed with buff moustache mark, finer breast streaks.

**Seasonal Abundance:** Common summer resident in region, rare in winter. Breeds across Canada, U.S., winters to Honduras.

**Where to Find:** Grasslands throughout region in summer. A few may linger in winter in open areas of southern Vancouver Island, Fraser Delta. Migrants occur out of habitat near open spaces, even in cities.

**Habitat:** Open grassland, agricultural fields, salt marsh, associated edges.

**Diet and Behaviour:** Forages mostly on ground for insects, seeds. Forms flocks, especially in migration, winter. Male sings from elevated perches.

**Voice:** Buzzy song of two to three longer notes followed by lower pitched, less clear buzzes. Calls include sharp, high, but quiet *pik*, thin *tsew*.

**Did you know?** Of the 17 recognized subspecies of Savannah Sparrow, one breeds in southwestern British Columbia while two others migrate through on the way to and from their northern breeding grounds.

**Date and Location Seen:** _____

Sooty

Slate-colored

**Description:** 16 cm. Bulky, **plain-faced** sparrow with **chevron-shaped spots** on whitish breast, reddish-brown tail, yellowish lower bill. Two distinct forms in region. SOOTY: Variably **dark chocolate-brown** to grey-brown with **dense markings below**. SLATE-COLOURED: **Grey on head, back** contrasting with rusty wings.

**Similar Species:** Song Sparrow (page 351) has grey eyebrow, all-dark bill. Hermit Thrush (page 313) has thin bill.

**Seasonal Abundance:** SOOTY: Common resident in region. Coastal; breeds Alaska to Washington, winters to California. SLATE-COLOURED: Fairly common summer resident in region in Cascade, Coast mountains in subalpine zone; rare in lowlands. Breeds mountains of northwestern North America, winters south to California.

**Where to Find:** SOOTY: Breeds on western Vancouver Island, central coast; winters throughout lowlands. SLATE-COLOURED: Manning Park, Whistler, Cypress Bowl, Garibaldi Park most accessible sites.

**Habitat:** In lowlands, brushy fields, forest edge including backyards; blackberry thickets, dense tangles preferred. Mountain breeding habitat subalpine meadows with small trees.

**Diet and Behaviour:** Forages mostly on ground for seeds, insects, some fruit. Scrapes ground with both feet, jumping forward, kicking back. Sings fall, spring in lowlands. Visits feeders.

**Voice:** Song rich, complex, melodic, staccato, lively. Calls include hard, smacking *chink*.

**Did you know?** Highly variable across its continent-wide range, Fox Sparrow is often treated as three or four separate species.

**Date and Location Seen:** _____

**Description:** 15 cm. Streaked brownish above with brown wings. **Dark, dense streaking** may merge into central spot on whitish breast. **Long, rounded tail pumped in flight. Wide grey eyebrow**, brown crown with grey central stripe, dark moustache mark. JUVENILE: Buffy below.

**Similar Species:** Fox Sparrow (page 349) lacks broad eyebrow. Savannah Sparrow (page 347), Lincoln's Sparrow (page 353) more finely streaked, trim-appearing. Swamp Sparrow (not shown; rare winter resident in region) plain grey below.

**Seasonal Abundance:** Common resident in region. Ranges across North America, south to northern Mexico.

**Where to Find:** Most abundant sparrow in region; found throughout, up to mountain passes.

**Habitat:** Prefers shrubs, thicket edge in wetter areas, but frequents all semi-open habitats, broken forest.

**Diet and Behaviour:** Feeds mostly on ground on insects, seeds (including below bird feeders), some fruit. Less prone to flock but can be gregarious in migration. Sings year round; in region, begins nesting in late winter.

**Voice:** Song begins with several clear notes followed by lower note, jumbled trill. Calls include distinctive nasal *chump*, thin *seet*.

**Did you know?** Over 30 subspecies of this highly variable sparrow have been recognized. Song Sparrows resident in our region are among the darkest. In migration and winter they are joined by other races, including a few lighter-coloured birds.

**Date and Location Seen:** _____

**Description:** 13.5 cm. **Small**, secretive. Streaked above, below. **Buff wash on breast with distinct fine, dark streaks that end abruptly** at clear white belly. Short tail, small bill, greyish face with divided brown crown, **buff moustache mark**, faint eye-ring.

**Similar Species:** Smaller than Song Sparrow (page 351), with buffy breast, finer streaks. Lacks white or yellow eyebrow of Savannah Sparrow (page 347).

**Seasonal Abundance:** Common migrant, fairly common in winter at lower elevations in region. Fairly common breeder in Cascades, May–September. Breeds from Alaska across Canada, south in western mountains; winters U.S. coasts, West Indies, south through Middle America.

**Where to Find:** Widespread in lowlands in winter. In summer, around Beaver Pond, Manning Park.

**Habitat:** Breeds in open meadows, bogs. Prefers wet, scrubby places at all seasons, but migrants use variety of habitats.

**Diet and Behaviour:** Feeds mostly on ground on seeds, insects, in or near cover. Less often in groups, but flocks with other sparrows.

**Voice:** Song fairly long series of bubbly musical trills, notes, generally given only on nesting grounds. Call sharp but soft chip.

**Did you know?** Lincoln's Sparrows are so inconspicuous in migration that they were formerly considered uncommon or rare. However, mist-netting at monitoring stations has shown them to be one of the commonest songbirds migrating along the coast.

**Date and Location Seen:** _____

Breeding

Immature

White-throated Sparrow

**Description:** 16.5 cm. Fairly large, long-tailed, with **unstreaked grey breast, black-and-white head stripes, yellowish-orange bill**. Faint white wing-bars, streaked back. IMMATURE: **Brown-and-grey head stripes**. JUVENILE: Streaked breast in summer.

**Similar Species: White-throated Sparrow** (see inset; uncommon in region in winter) browner, smaller, with **clearly marked white throat**. Golden-crowned Sparrow (page 357) has yellow forehead, dusky bill; immature with less defined head stripes.

**Seasonal Abundance:** Common summer resident in region, less common in winter. Breeds across northern North America, south to California in West; winters Pacific Coast, western, central U.S., to Caribbean, Mexico.

**Where to Find:** Nests throughout region up to mountain passes, including cities. Winters locally in lowlands, mostly in agricultural areas.

**Habitat:** Shrubby woodland edge, parks, cities. Farms, hedgerows preferred in winter.

**Diet and Behaviour:** Forages mostly on ground for insects, seeds, other plant material. Occasionally fly-catches from trees, bushes. Flocks with other sparrows.

**Voice:** Song begins with one to two whistled calls followed by rhythmic series of buzzy trilled notes. Calls include sharp *bink*, high, thin *seet*.

**Did you know?** Puget White-crowned Sparrow—the subspecies that nests in southwestern British Columbia—winters mostly in California. Almost all wintering birds are Gambel's White-crowned Sparrow, which breeds farther north.

**Date and Location Seen:** _____

**Breeding**

**Immature**

**Description:** 17 cm. **Large**, with **unstreaked grey breast**, long tail, relatively small **dusky bill**. Streaked brown above with **two white wing-bars**. BREEDING: **Golden crown bordered by black cap**. NON-BREEDING: Lacks black, has only hint of gold. IMMATURE: Resembles non-breeding.

**Similar Species:** White-crowned Sparrow (page 355) appears greyer, with orange-pink bill; adult has black-and-white head stripes (brown-and-buff in immature).

**Seasonal Abundance:** Common winter resident in region, arrives mid-September, departs by mid-May; very rare breeder in coastal mountains. Breeds from Alaska south through central British Columbia, winters along coast from southwestern British Columbia to northern Baja California.

**Where to Find:** In winter, lower elevations throughout region. Migrants also at high elevations.

**Habitat:** Brushy places, including neighbourhoods.

**Diet and Behaviour:** Forages on ground for seeds, insects, often in flocks with other sparrows. Also feeds in trees, shrubs on blossoms, buds, especially in spring. Occasionally fly-catches from trees, bushes.

**Voice:** Song whistled, mournful *oh dear me*, often given in migration. Call notes include thin *seep*, rich, loud *bink*.

**Did you know?** Golden-crowned Sparrows wander regularly as far as the East Coast.


**Date and Location Seen:** _____

Oregon
Male

Oregon
Female

Slate-colored

Juvenile

**Description:** 14.5 cm. Sparrow-shaped. Short **pink conical bill, white outer tail feathers**, whitish belly. Two distinct forms in region. OREGON JUNCO: Male with **black hood**, plain brown back; female duller with grey hood. SLATE-COLOURED JUNCO: Uniformly greyish with white belly.

**Similar Species:** Vesper Sparrow (not shown; rare in region) streaked above, below, lacks hood; other sparrows in region lack white outer tail feathers. Juvenile juncos streaked above, below, can be mistaken for sparrow but have white tail edges, pinkish bill.

**Seasonal Abundance:** Common resident in region; numbers increase in lowlands in winter. OREGON: Common year round (breeds, winters in West); SLATE-COLOURED: Small numbers appear in winter (breeds northern forests, winters throughout most of southern Canada, U.S.).

**Where to Find:** Throughout region; nests uncommonly in suburban areas.

**Habitat:** Nests in coniferous, mixed woods, especially brushy edges. In migration or winter can appear anywhere, including cities.

**Diet and Behaviour:** Flocks forage on ground, also in trees, mostly for seeds, insects. Often scratches at ground with feet. Regular beneath bird feeders.

**Voice:** Trilled song similar to that of Chipping Sparrow but more musical. Most common call sharp *tsip*.

**Did you know?** Oregon and Slate-coloured are but two of the many distinctive regional forms of the widely distributed, highly variable Dark-eyed Junco.

**Date and Location Seen:** _____

Male

Female

**Description:** 20 cm. Larger than most finches. **Plump**, square-tailed, with **large conical bill**. MALE: Adult with black head, tail, wings. **Wings, tail with bold white marks**. Breast, rump tawny brown. Immature without black head. FEMALE: Brown with little white in wings, tail. Strong **white head stripe, eyebrow, moustache mark**.

**Similar Species:** Evening Grosbeak (page 383) male with yellow eyebrow, female with plain head.

**Seasonal Abundance:** Common summer resident in region. Migrants (often seen in cities) arrive in May, first fall transients late July. Breeds in West, from southern British Columbia south through mountains of Mexico; winters Mexico.

**Where to Find:** Throughout region up to mountain passes.

**Habitat:** Nests mostly in mature deciduous or mixed forests away from urban areas, but in migration more widespread.

**Diet and Behaviour:** Insects, seeds, berries. Forages in trees. Occasional at bird feeders.

**Voice:** Melodious song long, whistled warble likened to "drunken robin." Distinctive call note, sharp *pik*, often reveals its presence.

**Did you know?** The Black-headed Grosbeak is not closely related to the Evening and Pine Grosbeaks. The latter species belong to the same family as crossbills and goldfinches, whereas the Black-headed is in a different family along with the Northern Cardinal of eastern North America.

**Date and Location Seen:** _____

Male

Female

# RED-WINGED BLACKBIRD
## *Agelaius phoeniceus*

**Description:** 22 cm. Medium-sized blackbird with fairly **stout, pointed bill**. MALE: **Glossy black with red shoulder patch** bordered with yellow-buff. FEMALE: Smaller; dark brown above, **heavily streaked** below with strong **buff eyebrow**.

**Similar Species:** Other blackbirds lack shoulder patch. Sparrows smaller than female Red-winged Blackbird, with more conical bill.

**Seasonal Abundance:** Common resident in region. In winter shifts from marshes to farms, retreats from higher altitudes. Breeds across continent south of Subarctic zone to Bahamas, Central America; leaves northern areas in winter.

**Where to Find:** Nests throughout region up to mountain passes in suitable habitat. In winter roosts in wetlands, but feeds more in agricultural areas.

**Habitat:** Marshes, meadows, brushy edge. Farms, feedlots in winter.

**Diet and Behaviour:** Seeds, insects. Forages mostly on ground but sometimes in trees. Flocks with other blackbirds. Often at bird feeders. During nesting, polygamous males protect their territory with frequent song, aggressively chasing out all intruders.

**Voice:** Main song of male *conk a ree*. Calls include *chek* note, rattles.

**Did you know?** Red-winged Blackbirds give more than 20 different vocalizations, a reflection of their complex social organization. Males have 18 different calls, females six. Four alarm calls are given by both sexes.

**Date and Location Seen:** _____

**Description:** 23 cm. Heavy-bodied, **short-tailed** member of blackbird family. Back, sides streaked brown. **Bright yellow underparts** with V-shaped black breast band. **Outer tail feathers white**. In flight, weak flapping alternates with gliding.

**Similar Species:** European Starling (page 319) lacks yellow underparts, white outer tail feathers.

**Seasonal Abundance:** Uncommon winter resident in region, rare in summer. Breeds from southern interior British Columbia to Michigan, south through Mexican highlands; winters from all but northernmost part of breeding range south to Gulf states, Mexico.

**Where to Find:** Eastern Vancouver Island, Lower Mainland in low-elevation meadows, agricultural areas. Reliable sites include Sea Island, Boundary Bay, Chilliwack, Martindale Flats, Nanaimo River estuary.

**Habitat:** Fields, prairies, farms; wet coastal habitats in winter.

**Diet and Behaviour:** Feeds on ground for insects, seeds. Probes soil with long, pointed bill. In winter usually in flocks. Often perches, sings high in trees, even during migration, winter; also sings from ground.

**Voice:** Song gurgling series of flute-like notes. Calls include *chupp*, rattle; thin, high buzz in flight.

**Did you know?** The Western Meadowlark was once a common breeding bird in the meadows of southwestern British Columbia, but numbers dwindled as urbanization replaced its habitat. The last known nesting record is from 1986.

**Date and Location Seen:** _____

Male

Female

**Description:** 23 cm. Medium-sized blackbird with **short, pointed bill**, fairly long, rounded tail. MALE: **Glossy blackish-green with purplish iridescent head, light yellow eye**. FEMALE: **Drab** grey-brown with dark eye.

**Similar Species:** Red-winged Blackbird (page 363) not as plain; female streaked, male with shoulder patch. Brown-headed Cowbird (page 369) smaller, bill more finch-like.

**Seasonal Abundance:** Common resident in region, but local. Breeds from British Columbia, Prairie provinces, to Great Lakes, California; winters in warmer parts of breeding range south to Gulf Coast, Mexico.

**Where to Find:** Patchily distributed around cities; much easier to find in agricultural areas.

**Habitat:** Pastures, feedlots, urban parking lots, other open places.

**Diet and Behaviour:** Mostly insects, seeds; also waste grain, crumbs. Forages mostly on ground, often in flocks—sometimes with other blackbirds, starlings. Visits bird feeders.

**Voice:** Courting male has *kseee* call. Year-round nasal *check* note.

**Did you know?** Nest-site selection by Brewer's Blackbirds varies greatly depending on local availability. They may build their nests in trees, on plant stalks over water, in low shrubs, on the ground in high grass, or even on rocky ledges.

**Date and Location Seen:** _____

Male

Female

Juvenile

# BROWN-HEADED COWBIRD
## *Molothrus ater*

**Description:** 19 cm. Small blackbird with **stubby conical bill**, relatively **short, square-tipped tail**. MALE: Black with **brown head**. FEMALE: Smaller, **plain** grey-brown, lighter below, with vague streaks. JUVENILE: Similar to female but paler, streaking more distinct.

**Similar Species:** Short bill, brown head distinguish male from other blackbirds. Female smaller than blackbirds, plainer than sparrows.

**Seasonal Abundance:** Common summer resident in region, most depart in winter. Breeds across North America from southern Yukon, Newfoundland, south through central Mexico; winters midwestern, southern U.S., Mexico.

**Where to Find:** Throughout region, including cities.

**Habitat:** Widespread in breeding season in woodlands, neighbourhoods, open areas. In migration prefers fields, farms.

**Diet and Behaviour:** Feeds on ground, mostly on seeds, insects. Does not build nest, instead lays eggs in other birds' nests. In breeding season groups of males display with odd postures, spread wings, noisily chase females. Flocks with other blackbirds after breeding.

**Voice:** Male gives gurgling squeaks in display. Female rattles. Flight call thin, high whistle. Juvenile begs from host species with *cheep*, given frequently.

**Did you know?** Brown-headed Cowbirds, once restricted to plains habitats, invaded more-forested regions as land was cleared for agriculture, settlement, and lumber production. Cowbird nest parasitism is now implicated in the decline of many forest songbirds.

**Date and Location Seen:** _____

Male

Male Immature

Female

**Description:** 20 cm. **Slim** with long tail, **tapered, pointed bill.** ADULT: Male orange with black cap, back, wings, eye-line, narrow bib, center of tail. **Large white wing patch.** Female duller, mostly grey-olive with whitish belly, **white wing-bars, orange wash on head, throat.** IMMATURE: Like female; male brighter with black throat.

**Similar Species:** Male unmistakable in region. Female Western Tanager (page 341) with heavier, blunter bill, lacks orange tones. Size, bill shape distinguish from warblers, goldfinches.

**Seasonal Abundance:** Uncommon, local summer resident in region. Arrives May, most depart by early August. Breeds southwestern Canada to Mexico, winters Mexico, Guatemala.

**Where to Find:** Fraser Valley, eastern Vancouver Island, e.g., Ladner Harbour Park, Colony Farm, Grant Narrows, Martindale Flats.

**Habitat:** Low-elevation deciduous or mixed woodlands with large shade trees—especially cottonwoods along rivers, but also open groves, parks, suburban neighbourhoods.

**Diet and Behaviour:** Forages in foliage of trees, bushes for insects, fruits, nectar from flowers. Sometimes visits hummingbird feeders. Weaves hanging, bag-shaped nest in outer limbs.

**Voice:** Series of rich, medium-pitched whistles, chatter. Calls include harsh *cshek*, rolling chatter.

**Did you know?** New World orioles such as Bullock's belong to the blackbird family. Early naturalists called them orioles because they superficially resemble the Golden Oriole of Europe, a member of an unrelated Old World family.

**Date and Location Seen:** _____

Male

Female

**Description:** 14.5 cm. Stocky finch with **short, notched tail, stout bill**. MALE: **Raspberry-red** on head, breast, extending to flanks, infusing brown back. Adult **without streaks on belly**. FEMALE: Brownish without red. Blurry streaks on whitish-buff breast, belly; undertail unstreaked. **Broad white eyebrow**.

**Similar Species:** House Finch (page 375) slimmer, male more orange-red with streaks on belly. Female lacks broad white eyebrow. Male Cassin's Finch (not shown; restricted to mountains on eastern edge of region) has scarlet crown, pink head, breast; female more crisply streaked beneath, including undertail.

**Seasonal Abundance:** Locally fairly common resident, migrant in region. Breeds northern forests, south in Appalachians, Pacific coastal mountains. Winters eastern North America, down Pacific Coast to Baja California.

**Where to Find:** Throughout region at low to mid-elevations, e.g., Pacific Spirit Park, Campbell Valley Park, Lighthouse Park, Miracle Beach Park, J.V. Clyne Nature Sanctuary, Rathtrevor Beach Park.

**Habitat:** Mixed woods, coniferous forest, semi-open areas with fruiting trees; more widespread in winter.

**Diet and Behaviour:** Forages on fruits, seeds, buds, some insects, mostly in flocks, especially outside nesting season. More arboreal than House Finch, but also feeds on ground. Uses bird feeders.

**Voice:** Series of warbled notes without harsh ending of House Finch song. Calls include muffled whistle, sharp *pik* given in flight.

**Did you know?** One-year-old male Purple Finches look like females—but unlike females, they sing.

**Date and Location Seen:** _____

Male

Female

**Description:** 14 cm. Sparrow-sized finch with long, only slightly notched tail. **Bill short, rounded**. MALE: Red (yellow in some individuals) on crown, breast, rump; **streaks on belly, flanks**. FEMALE: Brownish-grey without red. Blurry streaks on grey-white breast, belly. **No strong facial pattern**.

**Similar Species:** Purple Finch (page 373) more robust, adult male without streaks on lower breast, female with broad white eyebrow.

**Seasonal Abundance:** Common year-round resident in region. Ranges from southern Canada south through Mexico.

**Where to Find:** Throughout region, including cities, up to mountain passes.

**Habitat:** Urban neighbourhoods, parks, suburbs, farms, woodland edge. Avoids dense forest.

**Diet and Behaviour:** Often nests, feeds in backyards. Usually forages in flocks on ground, in weeds, or in trees for seeds, berries, blossoms, buds. Regular at sunflower feeders.

**Voice:** Series of cheery warbling notes often ending with harsh note. Call loud chirp.

**Did you know?** Native to deserts, scrublands, grasslands, and open forests of Mexico and the American West, House Finches extended their range as land was cleared for human settlement, first reaching southwestern British Columbia in the late 1930s. House Finches introduced to New York City in the 1940s have now spread throughout eastern North America.

**Date and Location Seen:** _____

Female

Male

**Description:** 15 cm. Compact finch with **large head, short, notched tail**, plain, dark wings. **Bill heavy with crossed tips**. MALE: Plumage variable; generally brick-red, sometimes orange, yellowish—brightest on crown, rump. FEMALE: Olive-yellow. JUVENILE: Dull, streaked.

**Similar Species:** Purple Finch (page 373), House Finch (page 375) smaller, less stubby, without crossed bill tips. Pine Grosbeak (page 393) larger with white wing-bars, uncrossed bill. White-winged Crossbill (not shown; rare in region) with white wing-bars.

**Seasonal Abundance:** Fairly common resident in region. Nests at any time of year. Movements occur through cities, generally April–May. Ranges worldwide, mostly above equator.

**Where to Find:** Erratic, nomadic. Localities, abundance vary with cone crops.

**Habitat:** Coniferous forest, mixed woods.

**Diet and Behaviour:** Flocks seek productive conifers, pry cones open, extract seeds. Also eats buds, other seeds, insects, minerals from ground. Occasional at bird feeders.

**Voice:** Song rapid series of hard chirps, warbles. *Kip kip* call given in flight.

**Did you know?** There are at least eight different forms of Red Crossbill in North America, each specializing in opening the cones of different trees. Most crossbills in coastal southwestern British Columbia have small bills adapted to the small cones of hemlocks.

**Date and Location Seen:** _____

**Description:** 12 cm. Upperparts streaked brownish, underparts buff-white with **well-defined, heavy, dark streaking**. Yellowish on wings, tail, not always visible on perched bird, but male's bold yellow wing stripe evident in flight. Tail notched. **Bill conical, long, pointed**.

**Similar Species:** Smaller than House Finch (page 375), Purple Finch (page 373); bill shape distinguishes from warblers, other finches. Common Redpoll (not shown; rare winter visitor in region) has black chin, red cap.

**Seasonal Abundance:** Common resident in region but can be scarce, local in late summer, fall. Breeds from Alaska across Canada, south through western U.S. to Guatemala; winters in all but northernmost part of breeding range, throughout U.S., Mexico.

**Where to Find:** Widespread in region, usually near conifers. Migratory, nomadic; local abundance varies unpredictably.

**Habitat:** Coniferous forest, mixed woods (especially with alders), weedy areas.

**Diet and Behaviour:** Gregarious. Feeds mostly in trees, but also on weed stalks, ground. Eats mostly seeds, but some insects taken. Large, compact flocks swirl noisily when alarmed. Flocks with other finches. Regular at thistle, black-oil sunflower feeders.

**Voice:** Song jumble of husky twitters, trills. Calls include rising *zreeee*, high, sharp *di di di*, both given in flight.

**Did you know?** Pine Siskins are susceptible to serious *Salmonella* infections—an important reason to keep your bird feeders clean.

**Date and Location Seen:** _____

Male Breeding

Female Breeding

Juvenile

**Description:** 13 cm. Variable plumage with **prominent wing-bars**, white undertail. **Short, conical bill**, pinkish in summer. BREEDING: Male **bright yellow** with black wings, forehead, tail. Female dull yellow, olive on back, with **blackish wings**. NON-BREEDING: Dull with some yellow on throat. JUVENILE: Browner on back with buff wing-bars.

**Similar Species:** Conical bill distinguishes from warblers; lack of streaks from sparrows, other finches.

**Seasonal Abundance:** Fairly common resident in region. Migratory; often difficult to find in winter. Breeds from southern Canada south to California, Oklahoma, Georgia; winters in all but northern fringe of breeding area, south through U.S. to Mexico.

**Where to Find:** Throughout region; less common in cities but frequents neighbourhoods, weedy lots.

**Habitat:** Weedy, open areas with some deciduous trees; farms, openings in forest.

**Diet and Behaviour:** Gregarious. Flocks most evident late summer, fall. Eats small seeds on weed stalks, especially thistles (favours thistle feeders in backyards), also in trees such as alder, birch, sometimes on ground.

**Voice:** Song long jumble of high, repeated twitters, phrases. Calls include *tee di di di*, mostly given in flight, thin *twee*.

**Did you know?** Since goldfinches feed their young seeds, they nest later than most other songbirds, often not beginning to lay eggs until early July.

**Date and Location Seen:** _____

Male

Female

**Description:** 20 cm. Plump, short-tailed finch with **massive conical bill**. Black wings, tail with **large white patches** on each. Bill green in spring, whitish in winter. MALE: **Bright yellow eyebrow**. Dusky brown head, chest grade to yellow belly, back. FEMALE: Brownish-grey with yellowish wash.

**Similar Species:** Black-headed Grosbeak (page 361) lacks yellow eyebrow of male, plain head of female. American Goldfinch (page 381) much smaller.

**Seasonal Abundance:** Fairly common in region in summer, less common, irregular in winter. Easiest to find in May, even in cities. Ranges across southern Canada, south in western mountains to Mexico; some southward movement in winter.

**Where to Find:** Widespread but local, mostly near coniferous woods. Less common nesting at low elevations.

**Habitat:** Primarily coniferous forest but also mixed woods.

**Diet and Behaviour:** Gregarious outside breeding season. Large flocks may forage together, mostly in trees, on seeds, buds including maple, ash. Also eats insects, fruit, comes to ground for gravel. Voraciously devours sunflower seeds at bird feeders.

**Voice:** Song repeated notes in series. Call strident, ringing *tcheew* given often by flocking birds.

**Did you know?** Although grosbeaks are generally thought of as seed eaters, Evening Grosbeaks often specialize in eating caterpillars during outbreaks of spruce budworms and other forest pests.

**Date and Location Seen:** _____

Male

Female

**Description:** 15 cm. An Old World sparrow, not closely related to native sparrows. **Chunky**, short-tailed, with **unstreaked** dingy grey breast, brown-streaked upperparts. MALE: Grey crown, **black face, bib**, with chestnut hind neck. Colours duller in winter. FEMALE: Plain, dull, with **light buff eyebrow**.

**Similar Species:** Finches of similar size streaked. Native sparrows not as compact. Harris's Sparrow (not shown; rare winter visitor in region) has pink bill, lacks chestnut on neck.

**Seasonal Abundance:** Common resident in region. Introduced from Europe to North America, most of world.

**Where to Find:** Throughout region, usually near human habitation.

**Habitat:** Cities, suburbs, farms. Flourishes in many inner-city areas that native species are unable to utilize.

**Diet and Behaviour:** Feeds on ground, often in flocks, mostly on seeds, insects, crumbs. Noisily roosts in thick bushes. Competes aggressively for cavity nest sites, much to detriment of native species. Regular at bird feeders.

**Voice:** Repeated series of *chirrup* notes. Chirping call often given by many birds simultaneously, creating cheerful din. Also rattles in excitement.

**Did you know?** Male House Sparrows get brighter as they begin nesting, not as a result of moulting, but through feather wear that reveals the attractive colours beneath.

**Date and Location Seen:** _____

_____

White-tailed Ptarmigan

American Three-toed Woodpecker

Blue Grouse

## WHITE-TAILED PTARMIGAN
### *Lagopus leucura*

Chicken-like bird of alpine meadows, rocky habitats above treeline. In summer, protectively coloured in brown, grey, buffy; white tail usually hidden. Male (shown) has white belly, bare red skin (sometimes concealed) above eye. Fairly common but furtive resident in high mountains of region; sits quietly, blends into background when intruders present. Winter birds pure white but seldom seen.

## BLUE GROUSE
### *Dendragapus obscurus*

Large chicken-like bird of coniferous forests. Tail with grey band at tip. Male (shown) upperparts mostly sooty-brown, underparts bluish-grey; female lighter, bluish tones muted. Absent from developed lowlands in region but fairly common in forested landscapes up to mountain treeline. Often detected by male's call, series of soft, deep, far-carrying hoots, from perch high in tree. Secretive in winter.

## AMERICAN THREE-TOED WOODPECKER
### *Picoides dorsalis*

Black-and-white woodpecker of subalpine forests. Compare Hairy Woodpecker (page 241). White back, flanks, barred with black. White moustache mark, line behind eye. Male (shown) has yellow crown patch. Uncommon resident in region in Cascade, Coast mountains; easily overlooked except when busily engaged in flaking bark from trees. Often concentrates in recently burned areas to exploit beetle infestations in standing dead timber.

Gray Jay

Horned Lark

Clark's Nutcracker

## GRAY JAY
### *Perisoreus canadensis*

Distinctive, small-billed jay of higher-elevation coniferous forests. Adult (shown) has dark grey upperparts, light grey underparts. Dark cap set off by light forehead, cheeks. Juvenile overall dark grey. Curious; begs from tourists, steals food in campgrounds. Often roams in family groups. Fairly common in intact, mid- to high-elevation coniferous forest throughout region. Rare in lowlands.

## CLARK'S NUTCRACKER
### *Nucifraga columbiana*

Distinctive relative of crows, jays, specialized for extracting seeds from pine cones. Medium grey with long, black, pointed bill. Wings black with white patch on inner trailing edge conspicuous in flight. Tail black with white edges. In region, fairly common but local resident at higher elevations in Cascades, eastern slopes of Coast Mountains, including Manning Park, Garibaldi Park, Whistler.

## HORNED LARK
### *Eremophila alpestris*

Small songbird of shortgrass habitats. Male streaked greyish-brown above, plain white below, with black breast band, mask, white eyebrow. Small, dark "horns" protrude from crown behind eye. Female (shown) paler, lacks horns. Fairly common summer resident of alpine meadows in region, rare in winter in lowlands. Widespread, highly variable species; individuals of other populations yellower on head, breast, sometimes found in lowlands, rarely nesting.

Mountain Chickadee

Boreal Chickadee

Mountain Bluebird Male

Mountain Bluebird Female

### MOUNTAIN CHICKADEE
*Poecile gambeli*

Chickadee of coniferous forests of interior. Very similar to Black-capped Chickadee (page 287) but with white eyebrow, sides, no white edging on wing feathers; rarely found in same habitat. *Chick a dee* call hoarser, slower; whistled song usually has four notes. Fairly common resident in region east of crest of Cascade, Coast mountains (Manning Park, Whistler). Very rare visitor to lowland feeders in winter, but may appear in numbers—possibly in response to mountain food shortages.

### BOREAL CHICKADEE
*Poecile hudsonica*

Chickadee of subalpine forests. Fairly common resident in region in mainland mountains above 1,500 metres elevation (e.g., Manning Park). Sometimes shares its montane haunts with similar Chestnut-backed Chickadee (page 289), Mountain Chickadee (this page), flocks with them outside nesting season. Boreal distinguished by buffy sides; grey-brown cap, back; distinctive, very nasal *si jay* call.

### MOUNTAIN BLUEBIRD
*Sialia currucoides*

Bluebird of dry, open country, parklands. MALE: Unmistakable in region: brilliant blue above, duller on breast, with white lower belly, undertail. FEMALE: Grey body with bluish wings, tail. In region, fairly common summer resident in subalpine zone on rain-shadowed east side of Manning Park. Rare but regular migrant through lowlands, especially spring.

Townsend's Solitaire

Gray-crowned Rosy-Finch

Pine Grosbeak
Male

Pine Grosbeak
Female

## TOWNSEND'S SOLITAIRE
### *Myadestes townsendi*

Ground-nesting thrush of higher-elevation forests. Slender, short-billed. Overall grey with prominent white eye-ring, white tail edges. Buffy wing stripe visible in flight, shows as small patch on folded wing. Fairly common but local summer resident in region in open forests, parklands of high Cascade, Coast, Vancouver Island mountains. In lowlands, uncommon spring migrant, rare fall migrant, winter resident.

## GRAY-CROWNED ROSY-FINCH
### *Leucosticte tephrocotis*

Chunky finch of high-mountain tundra. Bill fairly short, conical. Legs, feet black; bill yellow in winter, black in breeding season. Male (shown) mostly rich brown with pinkish tones on belly, rump, wings. Throat, forehead dark, rest of head grey. Female, juvenile duller. Fairly common breeder in remote, rocky clefts at edge of permanent snowfields on alpine meadows in region; easier to find in late summer when flocking. Rare visitor to lowlands in migration, winter.

## PINE GROSBEAK
### *Pinicola enucleator*

Large, long-tailed finch with heavy bill. ADULT MALE: Bright pinkish-red body, grey wings with two prominent white wing bars, grey tail. ADULT FEMALE: Grey body with yellowish or orangish head, rump; wings, tail like male. Fairly common resident in subalpine forests throughout region, descending in some winters to adjacent lowlands. Call loud, melodious *plit er eek* or *pu deep*. Often seen in small flocks, especially in winter.

**Black-footed Albatross**

**Pink-footed Shearwater**

**Northern Fulmar
Light Morph**

**Northern Fulmar
Dark Morph**

### BLACK-FOOTED ALBATROSS
*Phoebastria nigripes*

Large, chocolate-brown seabird, nests on islands in central, western Pacific. Common on open ocean west of Vancouver Island from late March through early October; rarely seen from land. Whitish face, heavy dark bill, white tail base; soars low over water on long, stiffly held wings (wingspan over two metres). Immature (shown) has dark tail base, duskier face. Other albatrosses rare in region. Shearwaters, gulls much smaller.

### NORTHERN FULMAR
*Fulmarus glacialis*

Gull-sized seabird, breeds in Arctic. Present year round on open ocean off Vancouver Island, smaller numbers in Juan de Fuca, Queen Charlotte straits. Two forms, both common in region. DARK MORPH dark grey, LIGHT MORPH white with grey wings, tail; both have white flash at base of outer flight feathers, small black smudge around eye, thick yellow bill. Flight style rapid flaps of stiffly held wings alternating with long glides—rather similar to shearwaters, very different from gulls.

### PINK-FOOTED SHEARWATER
*Puffinus creatopus*

Gull-sized seabird, nests on islands off Chile. Rare in spring, becoming fairly common by fall off west coast of Vancouver Island. Brownish-grey above, white below, pinkish bill. Underwings smudgy, dusky. Typical shearwater flight with stiffly held wings, arcing glides. Sooty Shearwater (page 397) smaller, dark below; Buller's Shearwater (not shown; uncommon in region) has clear white underwings, striking black markings on upperwing, dark bill.

**Sooty Shearwater**

**Fork-tailed Storm-Petrel**

**Red Phalarope Breeding**

**Red Phalarope Non-breeding**

## SOOTY SHEARWATER
### *Puffinus griseus*

Gull-sized, sooty-chocolate-brown seabird with dark bill. Nests on islands in southern oceans. Common spring–fall on open ocean west of Vancouver Island, smaller numbers in Juan de Fuca, Queen Charlotte straits. Conspicuous silvery-white panel on underwing at base of flight feathers. Flies low over water with short series of quick flaps followed by banked glide. Short-tailed Shearwater (not shown; less common fall–spring visitor in region) difficult to separate but usually with less white on underwing.

## FORK-TAILED STORM-PETREL
### *Oceanodroma furcata*

Small, grey, fork-tailed seabird, reminiscent of large swallow; common summer resident, rare in winter. Nests on islets off west coast of Vancouver Island, central coast, forages on open ocean. Blackish eye smudge, bill thick, short. Pale bar along upper wing surface, dark bar on underwing. Leach's Storm-Petrel (not shown; much less frequently seen in region) dark chocolate-brown with white rump.

## RED PHALAROPE
### *Phalaropus fulicarius*

Small Arctic-nesting shorebird; common spring, fall migrant offshore west of Vancouver Island, some years many remain through early winter. Often lands on water surface to feed. BREEDING: Unmistakable orange-red body, black-and-white head, yellow bill. NON-BREEDING: Pale grey above, white below, black eye patch, dark bill. Juvenile buffy with back mottled black. Red-necked Phalarope (page 173) very similar in non-breeding plumage but back more streaked, bill finer; juvenile has dark, striped back.

Pomarine Jaeger

Sabine's Gull

Black-legged Kittiwake
Adult

Black-legged Kittiwake
Immature

## POMARINE JAEGER
### *Stercorarius pomarinus*

Heavy, powerful, gull-like seabird. Nests in Arctic; common spring, fall migrant offshore west of Vancouver Island, very rare in Strait of Georgia. Dark chocolate-brown above, white below with dusky breast band (all-dark in dark morph, barred or dark in immature). Wings with white patch at base of outer flight feathers. Adult's central tail feathers elongated, spoon-shaped, twisted. Parasitic Jaeger (page 175), Long-tailed Jaeger (not shown; uncommon in region) slender-bodied, adults with longer, narrower central tail feathers.

## SABINE'S GULL
### *Xema sabier*

Small Arctic-breeding gull; common spring, fall migrant off west coast of Vancouver Island, rare in Strait of Georgia. Strikingly patterned black-white-grey wings. Bill black with pale tip; head dark grey (breeding), white with grey smudge behind (non-breeding). Immature: Brown above, tail black-tipped. Compare Bonaparte's Gull (page 177), Black-legged Kittiwake (this page).

## BLACK-LEGGED KITTIWAKE
### *Rissa tridactyla*

Small gull, nests along coasts in northern oceans. Fairly common year round, especially spring–fall, offshore or roosting on rocky shorelines along west side of Vancouver Island; rare in Strait of Georgia. ADULT: Wingtips appear as if dipped in black. Head white, grey smudge behind ear in fall, winter. Bill yellow, unmarked; legs, feet black. IMMATURE: Black "M" pattern on wings, black collar on back of neck, black bill, tail tip. Bonaparte's Gull (page 177) smaller, lacks black collar; compare also Sabine's Gull (this page).

**Arctic Tern**

Arctic Tern

Cassin's Auklet

Tufted Puffin

### ARCTIC TERN
*Sterna paradisaea*

Small, short-legged tern with long, forked tail; breeds in Arctic, Subarctic. Common spring, fall migrant offshore west of Vancouver Island, very rare in Strait of Georgia. Breeding (shown): black cap bordered below by white, scarlet bill, wingtips with narrow dusky edging. Belly, breast grey as back. Non-breeding: Bill black, forehead white. Immature: Barred grey above. Breeding Common Tern (page 195) has black tip to red bill, less grey on neck, breast; broader dusky edges on wingtips, shorter tail.

### CASSIN'S AUKLET
*Ptychoramphus aleuticus*

Dark grey, starling-sized alcid. Over 1 million pairs breed in British Columbia, about 80 percent of world's population. Common spring–fall on Juan de Fuca, Queen Charlotte straits, west coast of Vancouver Island, especially near breeding colonies; smaller numbers in winter. Pale belly, white eyespot; bill short, dark with pale base. Ancient, non-breeding Marbled Murrelets (both page 201) extensively white below; Rhinoceros Auklet (page 203) larger, browner.

### TUFTED PUFFIN
*Fratercula cirrhata*

Chunky, black-bodied alcid. Common May–October near breeding colonies along west coast of Vancouver Island, very rare in Strait of Georgia; almost never seen in winter as entire population moves far offshore. Breeding (shown): white face, large orange bill, long blonde plumes behind eye. Non-breeding: All-dark, bill smaller. Immature: Similar to non-breeding adult. Horned Puffin (not shown; very rare in British Columbia waters) white below, lacks plumes behind eye.

# Photographer Credits

The letters following the page numbers refer to the position of the photograph on that page (T = top, B = bottom, L = left, R = right, N = inset).

**Don Baccus**: 104T, 106. **Aaron Barna**: 200T, 278N. **Lee Barnes**: 46B, 54B, 74B, 84, 114, 130, 134, N, 146TL, 210, 214, 222B, 282T, 294, 326T, 386TR. **Tony Beck/VIREO**: 228B. **Brian Bell**: 30T, B, 34B, 198N, 236. **Rick and Nora Bowers**: 56T, 96N, 106N, 122T, 152N, 194T, 204B, 250, 264, 328T, 394BR, 396BL, BR, 400TL. **Keith Brady**: 30N, 90B, 112, 142, 212, 276B, 288, 368BL, 372T, B, 382T, B. **Jim Burns**: 176TL. **Steve Cannings**: 314B, 340B, 358TL. **Jane Cooper**: 116BL. **Mike Danzenbaker**: 200N. **Mike Donahue**: 126N, 182B, 184T, B, 186B, 190T, 398BR. **Mike Dossett**: 168BL. **Tom Eckert**: 82B, 120N, 156B, 160BR, 248, 282N, 290T, 332T, B, 346, 380N, 388TL. **Randy Findlay**: 272. **James R. Gallagher/Sea & Sand Audubon**: 376, 396TL. **Don Graham**: 72TR. **Carrie Griffis**: 376N. **Sherry Hagen**: 120. **Ned Harris**: 398TL. **Joe Higbee**: 100, 252, 344N. **Ralph Hocken**: 32T, 50T, 66T, 72BR, 76B, 78T, B, 146BR, 150T, 246, 274T, 296, 316T, B, 324T, 342T, 350, 354T, 362T, 366T, back cover. **Gloria Hopkins**: front cover, 244. **Julian Hough**: 394TR. **Peter LaTourrette/VIREO**: 342B. **Kevin Li**: 274B. **Jerry Liguori**: 130N, 132T, 194B, 268, 392TL, 400TR. **Dan Logen**: 238L, R, 380T. **Gary Luhm**: 42T, 62T, 140, 400BR. **Stuart**

**MacKay**: 60T, 138T, 152, 154T, 162BR, 168BR. **Sam Mann**: 218. **Dick McNeely**: 32B, 42N, 54N, 64, 94B, 122B, 124B, 126T, 256, 320, 348T, 356B. **Scott Mills**: 394BL, 398BL. **Tom Munson**: 122N, 128T. **Laure Wilson Neish**: 70B, 208, 226B, 354B. **Dennis Paulson**: 68T, 158B, 198T, B, 224N, 268N. **Jim Pruske**: 64N, 72TL, BL, 108T, 116BR, 118N, 136, 146TR, 162T, 202, 206, 216, 242T, B, 292, 318N, 322B, 356T, 358BR, 360T, B, 362B, 366B, 368T, BR, 370B, 380B, 384T, 386B. **Jim Robertson**: 36T, 266, 328B, 358TR. **Jim Rosso**: 112N, 284N. **Robert Royse**: 42B, 46T, 48B, 58B, N, 80T, B, 146BL, 150B, 154TN, 158T, 160BL, 164, 166T, B, 172T, 176TR, B, 178B, 190N, 222T, 230B, 232B, 344T, 352, 354N, 358BL, 364, 390BR. **Bart Rulon**: 36B, 38B, 40B, 60B, 86T, 108B, 162BL, 170, 178T, 286, 312, 374T, B, 384B, 394TL. **Margaret St. Clair**: 52T, 76T, 92T, 94T, 104N, 114N, 240L, 276T, 300. **Michael Shepard**: 34T, 144, 156T, 180T, N, 182T, 186T, 188T, N, 190B, 228T, 270N, 314T, 388B. **Brian Small**: 52B, 54T, 56B, 62B, 66B, 86B, 88T, B, 90T, 96T, B, 98T, 102, 104B, 128B, 148T, B, 168TL, TR, 180B, 188B, 192, 196B, 220, 226T, 236N, 240R, 242N, 254, 258, 260, 262, 280, 284, 290B, 298, 304, 310, 318T, 324B, 326B, 328N, 330T, B, 334, 336B, 338, 340T, 344B, 370N, 378, 392BL, BR, 400BL. **Patrick Sullivan**: 348B, 386TL. **Ruth Sullivan**: 200B, 230T, 388TR. **Hank Tseng**: 38B, 40T, 44T, 48T, 58T, 68B, 70T, 74T, 82T, 92B, 98B, 116T, 118T, B, 138B, 154B,

160N, 172B, 196T, 234T, 256N, 270, 308, 322T, 390TL, BL. **Idie Ulsh**: 154BN, 204T. **Barry Wahl**: 44B, 110, 278T, 302, 306, 318B, 336T. **Terry Wahl**: 396TR, 398TR. **Brian Wheeler**: 124T, 126B, 128N, 132B, 224, 322N. **Cathy Wise**: 370T. **Michael Woodruff**: 390TR. **Jim Zipp**: 36N, 174, 234B, 392TR. **William Zittrich**: 232T. **Tim Zurowski**: 50B, 160T.

---

The photos in this book were selected from images provided by professional and amateur photographers from across North America, including British Columbia. We invite bird photographers to contact us if they wish to submit new photos for our next edition. E-mail us at production@heritagehouse.ca with a brief description of the species you've photographed, and we will arrange for you to upload your images to a controlled site. Digital photos must have a minimum resolution of 300 dpi to be considered for inclusion.

# Index/Checklist of Southwestern British Columbia Birds

Use this checklist to keep a record of the birds you have seen. **Bold** numbers are for the main Species Account page.

Other Species Seen

_____

_____

_____

_____

_____

# Naturalist and veteran birder Bruce Whittington captures the birding experience in *Seasons with Birds*

This beautifully illustrated work takes readers through a year with birds, combining month-by-month descriptive information about birds with fascinating bird lore. A delight for anyone who appreciates the beauty and song of our feathered companions.

ISBN 1-894898-21-4
$26.95 CDN
$19.95 US
published by TouchWood Editions

# About the Authors

### RICHARD CANNINGS

Co-author of *Birds of the Okanagan Valley* and *British Columbia: A Natural History*; Program Coordinator for Bird Studies Canada, and former curator of the Cowan Vertebrate Museum at the University of British Columbia; now a consulting biologist living in Naramata, B.C.

### TOM AVERSA

Co-author of *Birds of the Puget Sound Region* and *Birds of the Willamette Valley Region*; records compiler for the Washington Ornithological Society, and member of the Washington Bird Records Committee; has worked at the Woodland Park Zoo since arriving in Seattle in 1996.

### HAL OPPERMAN

Principal author of *A Birder's Guide to Washington*; co-author of *Birds of the Puget Sound Region* and *Birds of the Willamette Valley Region*; past editor of the Washington Ornithological Society's journal, *Washington Birds*; has lived in the Seattle area since 1967.

# Short Index to Species

Use this index to find the main account for every species illustrated in the guide. A complete index is on pages 405–411.